HARRY BUERER

Following Christ

Rediscovering *the* Jewish Faith *of* Jesus

HigherLife Publishing & Marketing
   PO Box 623307
   Oviedo, FL 32762
   AHigherLife.com

Following Christ: Rediscovering the Jewish Faith of Jesus
Buerer, Harry
ISBN 978-1-958211-62-5 Paperback, 978-1-958211-63-2 Hardback
978-1-958211-64-9 eBook

Printed in the United States of America
10 9 8 7 6 5 4 3 2 1

THIS BOOK IS FOR

Christians who think Jesus' teachings are opposed to
Judaism, thus dismissing Judaism;

Jews who think that Jesus taught in opposition to Judaism,
thus dismissing Jesus; and

Anyone that might be a little bit curious. Welcome.

TABLE OF CONTENTS

There are many books that address Jesus' Jewish upbringing and culture, but most of them don't really deal with the religious side of the coin, namely Jesus' firm embrace of Judaism as his faith. This book focuses on that. In my view, understanding this is the key to understanding the New Testament writings.

HARRY BUERER

CHAPTER 1

What Do We Mean by Jewish Faith?

The thesis of this book is that Jesus practiced and taught the Jewish faith or Judaism. What do we mean by Judaism?

In the first century, there were several varieties of Judaism in existence, as exemplified by the Pharisees, Sadducees, and the Essenes in the Qumran community, just to name a few. After the temple was destroyed in 70 C.E., the Pharisees became the predominant leaders in Judaism. Today, there are also several varieties of Judaism, including Orthodox, Conservative, and Reform, their differences mostly based on how seriously they take the Scriptures.

The Scriptures used in Judaism since before the time of Jesus were the books of the Law, the Prophets, and the Writings, sometimes referred to as the "Old Testament." These were the books accepted by Jesus and the Jews of his time as Scripture.

Since the first century, several collections of Jewish traditions have emerged. These are written interpretations from rabbis about what the

Tanakh (Old Testament Scriptures) mean and how to observe them. Initially passed down orally, they were eventually written down, and are called the Mishna and the Talmud. These traditions, referred to as the "Oral Torah" to distinguish them from the written Torah (the five books of Moses) are considered authoritative by most forms of Judaism today.

. . . .

My contention is that Jesus essentially taught the Judaism current at the time, rather than introducing a brand–new religion and canceling all that had been revealed by God to Moses and the prophets.

. . . .

In this book, I'm assuming Judaism to include the core of what was revealed by God to Moses, the prophets, and the other writers of the Hebrew Scriptures, and I'm not taking a position on the collections of traditions. As far as I am concerned, Judaism in its simplest form, is the material contained in the biblical writings. Jesus may have embraced some of the nascent traditions, but I'm not assuming that. My contention is that Jesus essentially taught the Judaism current at the time, rather than introducing a brand–new religion and canceling all that had been revealed by God to Moses and the prophets.

What did this Judaism consist of? There are several key elements that make up the whole. Among these are God's embrace of Abraham and subsequently, the nation of Israel; Israel's calling to be God's special people; the giving in perpetuity of the land of Canaan for an inheritance; the "comprehensive set of instructions" (this is the meaning of the word *Torah*), given to the Jews regarding how to worship God and live their lives in ways that would separate them from the people of other nations;

and finally, the promise that God would never abandon them, but would eventually gather them from the nations where they had been scattered and establish them in the land He had promised them under the reign of King Messiah, a descendant of David, in Jerusalem.

What made Jesus' message unique was the fact that *he claimed to be this promised Messiah*. He offered the kingdom to those who would repent, turn away from their sin to follow God's instructions, and accept him as the promised King. If that had happened, the kingdom would have been established then and there.

Unfortunately, the leaders of Israel, the priests and teachers of the Law, did not repent and accept him as king. Instead, they arrested him and had him killed. At that point, plan B came into effect, which God had determined would actually occur from the beginning: Jesus functioning as a sacrifice to atone for the sin of all people, a thoroughly Jewish idea.

A close reading of the Gospels shows that Jesus embraced all of these Judaic themes. He practiced and taught the instructions given to the nation of Israel through Moses. He embraced the nation of Israel as God's special covenant people, and urged people to repent and accept the promised kingdom with him as the king.

After his resurrection, when the disciples asked him if he was now going to restore the kingdom, he basically said, "Not now, but later." He ascended back to His Father with the promise that he would return at some point and finish the job. In anticipation of that time, we can pray in the words he taught his disciples, "Thy kingdom come."

QUESTIONS

1. What is meant by the Jewish faith or Judaism?

2. What were some types of Judaism present in the first century?

3. What Scriptures were accepted by Jesus and the Jews of his time?

4. What practices did the Judaism of Jesus' time maintain?

5. What was the hope that Jews looked forward to?

6. Why did Jesus not establish the promised kingdom when he was on earth?

CHAPTER 2

Judaism as the Default

In my college theology class, the professor asked this question: "Was Jesus a Christian?" To most of us, the question seemed like circular reasoning. Our basic understanding of practicing Christianity was to follow the things that Jesus was understood to have taught. If a Christian is one who follows the teachings of Jesus, then certainly Jesus followed his own teachings, and was, by that definition, a Christian.

I suspect that our professor was trying to challenge us to think more deeply about the issue though. I'm not really sure what his preferred answer would have been, but if a Christian is defined as one who holds to the teachings of what came to be called Christianity, we definitely must think more deeply about the question. A great deal has changed over time.

By the second century, many people who called themselves "Christian" actually used the term *in opposition to Judaism*. If you were a Christian, you were, by definition, *not* an adherent of Judaism. What would Jesus have thought of this divide? On which side of it would he have stood?

If you think about it from another angle, the idea of Jesus being a proponent and practitioner of Judaism should be taken as the default assumption. The burden of proof should be on anyone who claims otherwise. Not the reverse.

If Jesus was really sent from God to convey his will to mankind, then you would expect this revelation from God to be in continuing agreement with God's prior revelations. This revealed Word of God was given by God to Moses and the prophets—the writings that represent Judaism. In this book, I will make the case that the message (and lifestyle) of Jesus and his early followers was totally in line with the teachings of the Hebrew Old Testament.

If that's the case, then why did this view ever stop being the default? If Jesus and all his immediate followers practiced and taught a Judaism that accepted Jesus as the promised King Messiah, how was that view ever replaced by one that says that following Jesus was not in line with Judaism? And how did this idea become so prominent so early in the history of the followers of Jesus?

There seem to have been several factors that contributed to this split between Judaism and what came to be called Christianity. I will highlight two that I think are of primary importance.

First, most of institutional Judaism had no use for the teachings of Jesus and His followers. They were very much against them. This is illustrated by the attitude of Saul of Tarsus, later (and better) known as Paul the apostle. As a Pharisee, he represented the core of Judaism and went to great efforts to stamp out the followers of Jesus. He obtained letters from the high priest authorizing him to go to all the synagogues in Damascus and arrest all who followed Jesus, taking them prisoner. (It's worth noting that these followers were found in the synagogues.)[1]

---

1 See Acts 9:2; 22:19; 26:11.

On this journey to Damascus, Paul saw a vision of Jesus, and realized that Jesus truly was from God and a bringer of God's message. Paul immediately made a 180–degree turn and devoted himself to preaching faith in Jesus. Nevertheless, he considered himself both a Pharisee[2] and a follower of "the Way"[3]—which was considered *a sect of Judaism*.

There were a number of Jews, representative of the temple priesthood, who opposed Paul's message and tried to have him killed.[4] Paul was arrested and put on trial before several Roman leaders in the process of appealing his case before Caesar. In each of these instances, Paul made the argument that he adhered to the same Judaism as his accusers, and they had no reason to accuse him, but that they were representing the broad thinking of most of Judaism in opposing the followers of Jesus.[5]

Over the years, the rabbis had developed prayers called the *Amidah* (or *Shemoneh Esrei*) for their people to follow. After the temple (and the temple worship with it) was destroyed in 70 C.E., the Jewish people scattered far and wide. In the absence of temple worship, those prayers were revived. Sometime during the early centuries after Jesus, the rabbis who were developing the Jewish liturgy added a "benediction" to those Eighteen Benedictions, which was actually a malediction against "heretics." This addition, the *Birkat ha–Minim*, states, "May no hope be left to the heretics." It is commonly understood that this particular prayer pointedly referred to the Jewish followers of Jesus, who were considered by that point in time to have abandoned the core of Judaism, along with any other enemies.

Since those in authority in mainstream Judaism considered the followers

---

2 See Acts 23:6.

3 See Acts 24:14.

4 See Acts 23:12.

5 See Acts 24:10–21; 25:8; and 26:2–23.

of Jesus a heretical sect, it was easy for those believers in Jesus at the time to distance themselves from the Jews that viewed them this way. However, the biggest factor in the shift of followers of Jesus abandoning any identification with Judaism (and much of God's prior revelation along with it) was an event that is often overlooked in first–century history: the *Fiscus Judaicus*, Latin for "Jewish tax."

After the Romans destroyed the temple in Jerusalem in 70 C.E. and scattered the Jews from Jerusalem, they still considered Jews as troublemakers, so they established an onerous tax on all the Jews, including the children, throughout the empire. The tax was the same amount the Jews had previously paid for the upkeep of their own temple; however, this money was going to a pagan temple instead, so it was doubly humiliating to the Jews. The determination of who was (or was not) subject to this tax was based on the person's lifestyle: Did they live in a Jewish manner? Gentile followers of Jesus would not have thought it fair to be taxed as Jews when they weren't Jews. They were just following God's commands for living and worshiping. However, following those commands looked very much like Judaism to the tax collectors, and they were not into splitting hairs.

As a result, there was strong motivation for Gentile Jesus–followers to distance themselves from Jews and their practices to avoid paying the tax. So they changed their day of worship from the seventh day of the week, Saturday, to the first, Sunday. They no longer gathered in synagogues and stopped celebrating the biblical festivals and feasts. They started referring to themselves as "Christians" and to their faith as "Christianity" in order to distance themselves from Judaism.

Key to this change was interpretation. They were able to find passages in the apostolic writings that they began to interpret as speaking negatively of Jews and their practice of keeping God's commands, the Torah. There were sections in Paul's writings, especially Galatians, which could be understood as downplaying Torah observance, even though Paul spoke highly of it in other writings, such as Romans. More on that later.

The writer of 2 Peter anticipated this issue and warned his readers that some of Paul's writings were confusing and hard to understand, and that some would pervert them and fall into the error of lawless men.[6]

By the third or fourth centuries, "Christian" writers were saying terrible things about Jews and their practices, and forbidding anyone from observing the seventh–day Sabbath God had commanded. Christianity had become essentially an anti–Jewish religion, and the greatest persecutors of Jews over the next several centuries would be Christians, especially after Christianity became the approved religion of the Roman Empire in the time of Constantine.

This prejudicial viewpoint and its subsequent distancing from Judaism has continued to this day.

What a vast change from a faith that had started as a legitimate branch of Judaism that considered Jesus as the promised King Messiah of Israel! This prejudicial viewpoint and its subsequent distancing from Judaism has continued to this day. Despite the Reformation and many variations in Christian doctrine, virtually none of the denominations of present–day Christianity have returned to the Judaism that was taught and practiced by Jesus and his disciples and early followers.

---

6 See 2 Peter 3:15–17.

QUESTIONS

1. What did God reveal to his people before the time of Jesus?

2. How did Jesus' message compare with prior revelation?

3. Why did some Jews oppose Jesus' claim to be Messiah?

4. Why do we tend to view Judaism as though it were in opposition to Christianity?

5. What two factors are mentioned that contributed to the split between Judaism and what came to be called Christianity?

6. How does Saul of Tarsus represent two opposing strands of Judaism?

7. Where did Saul go to find the followers of Jesus so he could arrest them?

8. What was Paul's response to the Jews who sought to have him killed?

9. What was the Roman tax on Jews called?

10. How did this tax give incentive to believing Gentiles to turn away from biblical practices?

11. What did the writer of 2 Peter say about Paul's writings?

12. What was "Christianity's" view of Judaism by the third or fourth century?

CHAPTER 3

Birth Prophecies and Narratives

There are two accounts of the birth of Jesus in the Gospels: one in Matthew and one in Luke. The other two Gospels pick up the story during Jesus' adult ministry. We will look at Matthew and Luke to see what they can tell us about Jesus' intended role.

Matthew 1 begins with an extended genealogy of Jesus through Joseph, his purported father. The summary of the genealogy emphasizes three points in Joseph's lineage: Abraham, David, and the exile to Babylon. The emphasis on Abraham seems to accent the fact that Jesus belonged to the people of Israel, God's chosen people.

The emphasis on David brings out the fact that Jesus was in the lineage of King David, to whom it was promised that his family would inherit the kingship of Israel forever. It's true that Jesus wasn't biologically related to Joseph, his adopted father; but in spite of that, it was through Joseph that Jesus' claim to the lineage of David came. And it was a legitimate claim. Adopted children received the rights of their parents.

The mention of the exile to Babylon primarily emphasized the need for restoration. The people of Israel had been promised an ultimate kingdom in their Promised Land under the reign of King Messiah. However, if they didn't follow God's instructions and turned to other gods instead, this kingdom would be delayed and they would be dispersed to other lands. After this and in God's time, they would be regathered and restored to their land under a king in the line of David. This is what the genealogy seems to point to: the expected restoration of Israel and reign of Jesus as their king.

After the genealogy, the account in Matthew goes on to tell that Mary was engaged to Joseph and found to be pregnant. While Joseph was deciding how to handle the situation, an angel appeared to him in a dream to assure him that the baby was from God. He should marry Mary and name the baby, "Jesus." The angel went on to say, "He will save his people from their sins."[1] This seems to refer mostly to His ultimate sacrificial death, but the use of the words "his people" identifies Jesus intimately with the people of Israel. These are not just his relatives. They are also his chosen people, his own, an entire nation for which he is responsible and one which only he can redeem. Here, as in Paul's epistle to the Romans, the salvation that Jesus' death provides is primarily for the people of Israel, and only secondarily for others.

In Matthew 2, we are told that at some point after the birth, magi came to Jerusalem, asking in Herod's court about one "born king of the Jews" because they had seen a star, and somehow surmised that it indicated the birth of the king of the Jews. Those familiar with Scripture knew of a prophecy in Micah 5:2 that said that a great king would be born in Bethlehem, the city of David. Herod told the wise men to let him know where they found this special child if they did. In reality though, Herod

---

1 See Matthew 1:21.

sent them to Bethlehem to find this newborn king, so that he could kill him.

After the magi found Jesus in a house with his mother, they avoided Herod on their return trip because God warned them in a dream not to go back to his court. When Herod realized that the wise men had returned to their home without conferring with him, he gave orders to kill all the male babies under the age of two in the vicinity of Bethlehem. However, after the magi had gone, an angel told Joseph to take his family into Egypt to escape Herod's wrath and stay there until told to return.

Matthew connects this event with a statement by the prophet Hosea who wrote, "When Israel was a child, then I loved him, and called my son out of Egypt" (Hosea 11:1 KJV). These words referred to the exodus from Egypt in the days of Moses, but Matthew related them to this occasion as well. The nation of Israel is often referred to as God's son.[2] In 2 Samuel 7:14, God speaks of a future king of Israel as His Son.

It's clear that in prophecy Jesus is uniquely connected with the nation of Israel as its representative. This is the point of the citation by Matthew in this connection. The nation was God's son, as was the promised king in the line of David: the role Jesus was expected to fill. Both were most precious to God.

It's also reminiscent of Isaiah's treatment of the servant of God. Sometimes the term referred to the nation of Israel as in Isaiah 41:8 and 49:3, while at other times, it referred to an individual who would not only gather Israel together,[3] but also suffer to pay for their sin as prophesied in Isaiah 52:13 to 53:12. The individual Isaiah referred to in these passages seems to have a unique connection with the nation of Israel, as the person

---

2 See Exodus 4:22, Deuteronomy 32:18, and Jeremiah 31:9 just to name a few.
3 See Isaiah 49:5.

named is referred to as *both* the servant and the son of God. Many times in the Gospels, especially in John, Jesus is referred to as the Son of God. This emphasizes his connection with national Israel, as well as with the line of Davidic kings.

The prophecies and narrative of Jesus' birth in the gospel of Matthew tie him very closely to the nation of Israel as a unique representative of that people, the One who will provide them salvation, as well as reign over them in the promised kingdom.

Luke provided even more details that tied Jesus to the life and worship of the people of Israel and the instructions God gave them. In the first chapter, we learn about the birth of Jesus' relative, John the Baptist. The chapter begins by emphasizing the obedient lifestyle of Zechariah, a priest, and his wife, Elizabeth. They are commended for "walking in all the commandments and ordinances of the Lord blameless" (Luke 1:6 KJV). It's clear that at least this side of the family was deeply immersed in biblical Judaism, and they are strongly commended by Luke, the author of the gospel.

An angel appears to Zechariah to herald John's birth. In the angel's prophecy, several things are mentioned about John's future role. He is never to take wine or other fermented drink, which makes him, like Samson in Judges 13:7, a lifelong Nazirite. The laws of the Nazirite are detailed in Numbers 6, but they were typically voluntary—a vow that someone took to intentionally draw near to God for a period of time. During that time, the Nazirite doesn't eat grapes or drink grape juice or wine, and doesn't cut his hair. At the end of this period, he cuts off his hair and offers specific offerings.

The apostle Paul seems to have taken such a vow.[4] He also paid the

---

4 See Acts 18:18.

expenses for others to go through this process in order to prove to people that he was living in obedience to the Law when he visited Jerusalem.[5] The laws of the Nazirite are clearly part of the Mosaic Law, and were enthusiastically embraced by John, as well as Jesus' later follower, Paul.

Another detail that's given about John's future is this:

"And he will turn many of the sons of Israel back to the Lord their God. And it is he who will go as a forerunner before Him in the spirit and power of Elijah, to turn the hearts of fathers back to their children, and the disobedient to the attitude of the righteous, to make ready a people prepared for the Lord." (Luke 1:16–17)

Clearly this calling is to advance God's teachings given in the writings of Moses and the prophets and to encourage people to follow the commands that God gave them in those Scriptures.

Also in this chapter (and preceding the birth of John), an angel appeared to Mary bringing the news of the child she would bear. The passage makes a point of saying that Joseph, Mary's intended, was a descendant of David. The only reason for pointing this out is to show the baby's qualification for kingship over Israel. The angel goes on to say:

"He will be great and will be called the Son of the Most High; and the Lord God will give Him the throne of His father David; and He will reign over the house of Jacob forever, and His kingdom will have no end." (Luke 1:32–33)

Once again, we see the theme of the king of Israel being called a son of God. He is to be given the throne of David and eternal reign over

---

5 See Acts 21:17–26.

the house of Jacob. This can only refer to the ultimate kingdom of Israel described by the prophets.

Later, when Mary visited Elizabeth, she recited a song about how God had blessed her. Part of that song included the blessings of her promised Son to Israel.

"He has given help to His servant Israel, in remembrance of His mercy, as He spoke to our fathers, to Abraham and his descendants forever." (Luke 1:54–55)

By these words, Jesus was recognized as the representative and benefactor of the people of Israel.

After John was born, he was circumcised on the eighth day, another indication that his family strictly observed their Jewish faith. Then his father, Zechariah, gave a divine prophecy that praised God for visiting and redeeming Israel and for John's future role in preparing the way and bringing the people back to God.

The most familiar part of Jesus' birth narrative is in Luke 2, as it's reviewed every Christmas. Joseph and Mary traveled from Nazareth to Bethlehem to pay a Roman tax because of Joseph's lineage through David. We've already seen that the prophet Micah predicted that the ultimate ruler of Israel would be born in Bethlehem. After the baby was born and laid in a manger, an angel appeared to a group of shepherds in the fields near Bethlehem. The angel described the new baby as a Savior, and also as Christ (Messiah) the Lord. The shepherds searched and found the baby as described, and then returned to their flocks, praising God. They would have been familiar with the prophecies about the Messiah, the ultimate Son of David who would rule Israel forever. They knew what this birth portended for their nation. Imagine their excitement and anticipation. For them, this meant not only an end to the oppression of the Roman Empire, but also freedom for every slave in the world, and much, much more. Messiah would usher in a time of complete joy and happiness as well as worldwide peace. All of these ideas were firmly rooted in the Word of God that they had been reading and following for a long time!

On the eighth day of Jesus' life, he was circumcised, as commanded in Genesis 17 for all the descendants of Abraham, and he was given the name "Jesus" (probably *Yeshua* in Hebrew) meaning "salvation" as the angel had instructed.

Since Jesus was a firstborn male, the family was obligated under the Law to consecrate him to God and pay an offering.[6] A new mother had to wait thirty–three days after the birth to be considered purified before she could go into the temple. After waiting for this period, Joseph and Mary took the baby to the temple in Jerusalem, a short trip from Bethlehem, for the consecration ceremony.

While passing through the temple courts, they encountered two people who made prophetic utterances about the baby Jesus. One was a man named Simeon, who had been told by the Holy Spirit that he would not die until he had seen the Messiah, the ultimate King of Israel. When he saw Jesus, he rejoiced that God had kept His promise, saying, "For my eyes have seen Your salvation, which You have prepared in the presence of all the peoples: a light for revelation for the Gentiles, and the glory of Your people Israel" (Luke 2:30–32). He went on to tell Mary this: "Behold, this Child is appointed for the fall and rise of many in Israel, and as a sign to be opposed—and a sword will pierce your own soul—to the end that thoughts from many hearts may be revealed" (Luke 2:34–35).

This pronouncement by Simeon referenced both the ultimate reign of

---

6 See Exodus 13:1–2, 11–15.

Jesus and his sacrificial death. It also tied him very closely to the people of Israel.

The other voice in the temple was that of a widowed prophetess, Anna, who spent all her time in the temple. The text says she spoke about the child to all who were looking forward to the redemption of Jerusalem. This is an allusion to prophecies like Isaiah 52:9, which look forward to the restoration of the kingdom of God centered in Jerusalem.

The passage concludes by stating, "And when His parents had completed everything in accordance with the Law of the Lord, they returned to Galilee, to their own city of Nazareth" (Luke 2:39). This emphasizes the fact that Jesus' family—like John's—carefully followed the commands of God given through Moses that are at the heart of Judaism.

The remainder of Luke 2 deals with an incident when Jesus was twelve years old. In response to the command in Deuteronomy 16:16 that said that all males must attend the Passover in Jerusalem, the family traveled there to celebrate the feast. Young Jesus gravitated to the temple, which he called his Father's house. He spent several days there conversing with the rabbis and asking them questions. This building which was the central point of Judaism was also the central point of Jesus' life on His visit to Jerusalem as a youth just as it would be in his future visits as an adult. Can there be any doubt that Judaism was the faith and worship Jesus embraced, seeing that it was based on God's prior revelation to his people?

QUESTIONS

1. Which two gospels talk specifically about the birth of Jesus?

2. How was Jesus descended from King David?

3. How does baby Jesus' trip to Egypt and back represent the nation of Israel?

4. What other people or entities in Scripture are referred to as God's "son"?

5. When an angel appeared to Mary, what did he say about the reign of Jesus?

6. In what ways did Jesus' family specifically obey the Law of Moses regarding his birth and early days?

7. How was Jesus representative of the nation of Israel?

The Prophesied Kingdom

The purpose of this chapter is to show how often the ultimate future kingdom of Israel is mentioned in the Old Testament and what the Jews were rightly expecting from one claiming to be the Messiah. We will also touch on some teachings that aren't exactly prophecies, but relate to the promise of the kingdom anyway.

When God called Abraham, He promised to make him and his descendants into a great nation.[1] Similar promises are made to his son Isaac,[2] and to Isaac's son Jacob.[3] The first specific mention of a king and a kingdom comes when Jacob blesses his sons on his deathbed. After some rather negative comments about his older sons, Jacob gets around to speaking of his son, Judah.

"As for you, Judah, your brothers shall praise you; your hand shall be on the neck of your enemies; your father's sons shall bow down to you.

---

1 See Genesis 12:2.

2 See Genesis 26:24.

3 See Genesis 28:13–15.

Judah is a lion's cub; from the prey, my son, you have gone up. He crouches, he lies down as a lion, and as a lion, who dares to stir him up? The scepter will not depart from Judah, nor the ruler's staff from between his feet, until Shiloh comes, and to him shall be the obedience of the peoples. He ties his foal to the vine, and his donkey's colt to the choice vine; he washes his garments in wine, and his robes in the blood of grapes. His eyes are dull from wine, and his teeth white from milk. (Gen. 49:8–12)

This is where the idea of the Lion of the Tribe of Judah originated. This metaphor is ultimately used of Jesus in Revelation 5:5, but what really stands out here in this blessing is verse 10: "The scepter will not depart from Judah, nor the ruler's staff from between his feet, until Shiloh comes, and to him shall be the obedience of the peoples." This prediction definitely points to a specific future ruler to whom the scepter belongs. This ultimate ruler is clearly predicted to come from the tribe of Judah. It even hints at a worldwide rule, since it speaks of all people obeying him. This same attitude is echoed in Psalm 2:

> *This prediction definitely points to a specific future ruler to whom the scepter belongs.*

Why are the nations restless and the peoples plotting in vain? The kings of the earth take their stand and the rulers conspire together against the Lord and against His Anointed. (Psalm 2:1–2)

Here we have the nations conspiring against the Lord and His Messiah (the meaning of "anointed"). God has installed His king in Zion

(Jerusalem) and refers to this Messiah as His Son. This Son will rule the nations with an iron scepter and dash them to pieces like pottery. It's a clear picture of a king appointed by God to reign in Jerusalem with a worldwide reach.

Before we go on to more promises and prophecies of this kingdom, let's go back to Genesis and study the life of Joseph as it has many parallels to the life of Jesus and his projected future return. The life of Joseph is covered in Genesis 37–50. It is neatly divided into two segments: his younger life with his family, and his later life in Egypt. In his youth, Joseph was a shepherd, favored above his brothers by his father because he was the son of Jacob's favorite wife, Rachael, who later died giving birth to his younger brother, Benjamin.

Joseph had dreams. He saw sheaves and stars bowing down to him in his dreams and made the mistake of sharing his dreams with his family. There was clearly a hint of royalty to those dreams, but his brothers rejected that idea completely. One day, they saw Joseph coming from afar and planned to kill him, but Reuben convinced them to throw him into a pit instead, planning to rescue him later, but that didn't work out. Joseph was as good as dead in this situation. While Reuben was away, Judah pulled Joseph out of the pit and sold him to traders on their way to Egypt. Reuben was grief–stricken; but in the end, they killed a goat, dipped Joseph's coat in its blood, and took it to their father, claiming that Joseph was killed by wild animals, which broke his heart.

But Joseph was not dead. Through a series of misadventures in Egypt during which Joseph never faltered in his faith and trust in God, he eventually successfully interpreted dreams for Pharaoh himself. Pharaoh made Joseph second–in–command in the kingdom, and was put in charge of the food in preparation for the famine foretold in Pharaoh's dreams. So Joseph frugally managed the food, saving a percentage every year so the people would be able to make it through the rough time ahead. When the expected famine hit, it was massive. Eventually Joseph's brothers came to Egypt to get food. Joseph played a dual role as ruler and savior (from starvation) in this situation. When they came, his brothers didn't even recognize him. Joseph didn't immediately share his identity, but carefully managed them.

Finally Joseph revealed himself to his brothers. Of course, they were terrified. They had treated Joseph despicably, and here he was, standing before them as the very ruler he had seen in his dreams—and with the power to kill every one of them. But that's not what Joseph does. Instead he assures them of his forgiveness and brings the whole family to live with him, rejoicing to see his father and younger brother again. In fact, Joseph sets them up in the richest section in Egypt. If Jesus is indeed the promised Messiah, the parallels here are hard to miss.

Now let's move to the time of King David. Saul was the first king of Israel, but not long after he began, he disobeyed God's commands and was rejected as king. Samuel, the priest and prophet, was commanded by God to anoint David as the next king, even though he was just a shepherd lad, the youngest of his brothers. However, as circumstances worked out, David became king over all Israel, and his reign was the high point in the history of Israel.

It was David that had the idea to build a more permanent house for God to replace the tabernacle. God sent the prophet Nathan to tell David that he would not be the one to build it, and went on to reveal God's eternal promises regarding David and his descendants.

Now then, this is what you shall say to My servant David: "This is what the Lord of armies says: 'I Myself took you from the pasture, from following the sheep, to be leader over My people Israel. And I have been with you wherever you have gone, and have eliminated all your enemies from you; I will also make a great name for you, like the names of the great men who are on the earth. And I will establish a place for My people Israel, and will plant them, so that they may live in their own place and not be disturbed again, nor will malicious people oppress them anymore as previously, even from the day that I appointed judges over My people Israel; and I will give you rest from all your enemies. The Lord also declares to you that the Lord will make a house for you. When your days are finished and you lie down with your fathers, I will raise up your descendant after you, who will come from you, and I will establish his kingdom. He shall build a house for My name, and I will establish the throne of his kingdom forever. I will be a father to him and he will be a son to Me; when he does wrong, I will discipline him with a rod of men and with strokes of sons of mankind, but My favor shall not depart from him, as I took it away from Saul, whom I removed from you. Your house and your kingdom shall endure before Me forever; your throne shall be established forever.'" (2 Sam. 7:8–16)

This is an amazing promise. It involves a permanent land for the people of Israel and an era of peace. It asserts that David's son will build the house for God, and will be given an eternal throne. It identifies David's son as God's son, and promises David that his house, kingdom, and throne will be established *forever.*

These promises obviously didn't come to pass immediately. David's son Solomon did build the temple, but many of the subsequent kings displeased God. Soon after Solomon's death, the kingdom was divided, and both halves were sent into exile by outside empires over the next several centuries. During the exiles, God raised up prophets to call for repentance, and assure the people of Israel that what God had promised them was still in the cards.

Virtually all the prophets whose writings are part of Scripture predicted this ultimate future kingdom, with the possible exception of Jonah. Before we go on to the later prophets, however, let's go back to Deuteronomy 30 and see a prediction given by Moses that acts as a kind of foundation for the later prophecies.

Moses had just predicted that the people of Israel would sin and turn away from God, but nevertheless, he predicts a time when God will gather them back to the land again:

So it will be when all of these things have come upon you, the blessing and the curse which I have placed before you, and you call them to mind in all the nations where the Lord your God has scattered you, and you return to the Lord your God and obey Him with all your heart and soul in accordance with everything that I am commanding you today, you and your sons, then the Lord your God will restore you from captivity, and have compassion on you, and will gather you again from all the peoples where the Lord your God has scattered you. If any of your scattered countrymen are at the ends of the earth, from there the Lord your God will gather you, and from there He will bring you back. The Lord your God will bring you into the land which your fathers possessed, and you shall possess it; and He will be good to you and make you more numerous than your fathers. Moreover, the Lord your God will circumcise your heart and the hearts of your descendants, to love the Lord your God with all your heart and all your soul, so that you may live. And the Lord your God will inflict all these curses on your enemies and on those who hate you, who persecuted you. And you will again obey the Lord, and follow all

His commandments which I am commanding you today. Then the Lord your God will prosper you abundantly in every work of your hand, in the children of your womb, the offspring of your cattle, and in the produce of your ground, for the Lord will again rejoice over you for good, just as He rejoiced over your fathers; if you obey the Lord your God, to keep His commandments and His statutes which are written in this Book of the Law, if you turn to the Lord your God with all your heart and soul. (Deuteronomy 30:1–10)

The high points of this prophecy are several: a return to the Lord and His commands; a regathering from countries of exile to the Promised Land; an internalization of loving and obeying God; and a prosperity in agriculture and the growth of families. Many of these things would be repeated in the predictions of later prophets.

As we know, there were eventually kings over both Israel and Judah. Some of them were godly and led the people back to Torah. Some of them were not, and turned the people away from God's commands. Over time, more and more of the kings were bad and the people turned away from God and followed the religions of the Baals around them. Of course, this was met with God's judgment, and a series of exiles. These judgments included the captivity of the Israelite people along with the destruction of Solomon's temple by the Babylonians under Nebuchadnezzar in 586 B.C.E.

Finally, in the time of Jeremiah, the people of Judah were exiled. After forty years, some of the people were allowed to come back and rebuild the temple and the city of Jerusalem. But most of them remained in exile. During this time God sent prophets to explain why they were in exile, calling them to return to God. Much of the message of these prophets involved a future regathering of the people and the establishment of a renewed kingdom of Israel with Jerusalem as its capital ruled by a representative of David, and following God's laws completely. We will look at these prophets and what they have to say about this future kingdom and the One who would rule over it.

The prophet Isaiah has much to say about this future time of blessedness for the nation of Israel. Here's a sampling:

> *Now it will come about that in the last days the mountain of the house of the Lord will be established as the chief of the mountains, and will be raised above the hills; and all the nations will stream to it. And many peoples will come and say, "Come, let's go up to the mountain of the Lord, to the house of the God of Jacob; so that He may teach us about His ways, and that we may walk in His paths." For the law will go out from Zion and the word of the Lord from Jerusalem. And He will judge between the nations, and will mediate for many peoples; and they will beat their swords into plowshares, and their spears into pruning knives. Nation will not lift up a sword against nation, and never again will they learn war. (Isa. 2:2–4)*

The emphasis here is the location—the mountain of Zion in Jerusalem and the coming of all nations (not just Israel) to that mountain. The other emphases are the Law of God being the standard of behavior and the peaceful coexistence of the nations.

In Isaiah 9, we are told of the birth of a child who would be the ruler of this kingdom.

> *For a Child will be born to us, a Son will be given to us; and the government will rest on His shoulders; and His name will be called Wonderful Counselor, Mighty God, Eternal Father, Prince of Peace. There will be no end to the increase of His government or of peace on the throne of David and over his*

kingdom, to establish it and to uphold it with justice and righteousness from then on and forevermore. The zeal of the Lord of armies will accomplish this. (Isa. 9:6–7)

This "Prince of Peace" will reign on David's throne forever. This is the role of Messiah, the anointed king.

Isaiah 11 is entirely about this future kingdom. It focuses first on the king who will be from the line of David.

Then a shoot will spring from the stem of Jesse, and a Branch from his roots will bear fruit. The Spirit of the Lord will rest on Him, the spirit of wisdom and understanding, the spirit of counsel and strength, the spirit of knowledge and the fear of the Lord. And He will delight in the fear of the Lord, and He will not judge by what His eyes see, nor make decisions by what His ears hear; but with righteousness He will judge the poor, and decide with fairness for the humble of the earth; and He will strike the earth with the rod of His mouth, and with the breath of His lips He will slay the wicked. Also righteousness will be the belt around His hips, and faithfulness the belt around His waist. (Isa. 11:1–5)

Next, it goes on to express the peace among animals based on a universal knowledge of the Lord. This has often been taken as a metaphorical picture of Israel living in peace with other nations.

And the wolf will dwell with the lamb, and the leopard will lie down with the young goat, and the calf and the young lion and the fattened steer will be together; and a little boy will lead them. Also the cow and the bear will graze, their young will lie down together, and the lion will eat straw like the ox. The nursing child will play by the hole of the cobra, and the weaned child will put his hand on the viper's den. They will not hurt or destroy in all My holy mountain, for the earth will be full of the knowledge of the Lord As the waters cover the sea. (Isa. 11:6–9)

Then it returns to the person of the Messiah, and explains how all nations will rally to him.

Then on that day the nations will resort to the root of Jesse, who will stand as a signal flag for the peoples; and His resting place will be glorious. Then it will happen on that day that the Lord will again recover with His hand the second time the remnant of His people who will remain, from Assyria, Egypt, Pathros, Cush, Elam, Shinar, Hamath, and from the islands of the sea. And He will lift up a flag for the nations and assemble the banished ones of Israel, and will gather the dispersed of Judah from the four corners of the earth. (Isa. 11:10–12)

In chapter 14, the emphasis goes back to the people of Israel and the land of Israel, as well as their relation to other nations.

When the Lord has compassion on Jacob and again chooses Israel, and settles them on their own land, then strangers will join them and attach themselves to the house of Jacob. The peoples will take them along and bring them to their place, and the house of Israel will make them their own possession in the land of the Lord as male and female servants; and they will take their captors captive and will rule over their oppressors. (Isa. 14:1–2)

In chapter 16, there is another mention of this king from the line of David:

A throne will be established in faithfulness, and a judge will sit on it in

trustworthiness in the tent of David; moreover, he will seek justice, and be
prompt in righteousness. (Isa. 16:5)

Over in chapter 24, Isaiah discussed the devastation of the earth, but in chapter 25, he discussed a banquet the Lord would prepare and the destruction of death itself.

Now the Lord of armies will prepare a lavish banquet for all peoples on this mountain; a banquet of aged wine, choice pieces with marrow, and refined, aged wine. And on this mountain He will destroy the covering which is over all peoples, the veil which is stretched over all nations. He will swallow up death for all time, and the Lord God will wipe tears away from all faces, and He will remove the disgrace of His people from all the earth; for the Lord has spoken. (Isa. 25:6–8)

Virtually all of Isaiah 25–27 relates to the establishment of this kingdom and praises God for it. However, there is a significant passage at the end of chapter 27 that might give some context to Paul's later writing in 1 Thessalonians 4:16–17 and 1 Corinthians 15:51–52.

On that day the Lord will thresh from the flowing stream of the Euphrates River to the brook of Egypt, and you will be gathered up one by one, you sons of Israel. It will come about also on that day that a great trumpet will be blown, and those who were perishing in the land of Assyria and who were scattered in the land of Egypt will come and worship the Lord on the holy mountain in Jerusalem. (Isa. 27:12–13)

There's another mention of the king and Jerusalem in chapter 33:

Your eyes will see the King in His beauty; they will see a distant land....

Look at Zion, the city of our appointed feasts; your eyes will see Jerusalem, an undisturbed settlement, a tent which will not be folded; its stakes will never be pulled up, nor any of its ropes be torn apart. But there the majestic One, the Lord, will be for us a place of rivers and wide canals on which no boat with oars will go, and on which no mighty ship will pass—for the Lord is our judge, the Lord is our lawgiver, the Lord is our king; He will save us— (Isa. 33:17, 20–22)

The entirety of chapter 35 is a familiar passage about agriculture flourishing, sickness vanishing, and animals living in peace. The chapter ends with "and the redeemed of the LORD will return and come to Zion with joyful shouting, and everlasting joy will be on their heads. They will obtain gladness and joy, and sorrow and sighing will flee away" (Isa. 35:10).

Moving over to chapter 52, we see why people refer to this future time as the redemption of Jerusalem.

How delightful on the mountains are the feet of one who brings good news, who announces peace and brings good news of happiness, who announces salvation, and says to Zion, "Your God reigns!" Listen! Your watchmen raise their voices, they shout joyfully together; for they will see with their own eyes when the Lord restores Zion. Be cheerful, shout joyfully together, you ruins of Jerusalem; for the Lord has comforted His people, He has redeemed Jerusalem. The Lord has bared His holy arm in the sight of all the nations, so that all the ends of the earth may see the salvation of our God. (Isa. 52:7–10)

Chapter 62 refers to asking God, as Jesus taught his disciples, to establish this kingdom.

On your walls, Jerusalem, I have appointed watchmen; all day and all night they will never keep silent. You who profess the Lord, take no rest for yourselves; and give Him no rest until He establishes and makes Jerusalem an object of praise on the earth. The Lord has sworn by His right hand and by His mighty arm: "I will never again give your grain as food for your enemies, nor will foreigners drink your new wine for which you have labored." But those who harvest it will eat it and praise the Lord; and those who gather it will drink it in the courtyards of My sanctuary. (Isa. 62:6–9)

As the book of Isaiah draws to a close, we see a lengthy description of the prosperity of this kingdom in chapter 65.

"For behold, I create new heavens and a new earth; and the former things will not be remembered or come to mind. But be glad and rejoice forever in what I create; for behold, I create Jerusalem for rejoicing and her people for gladness. I will also rejoice in Jerusalem and be glad in My people; and there will no longer be heard in her the voice of weeping and the sound of crying. No longer will there be in it an infant who lives only a few days, or an old person who does not live out his days; for the youth will die at the age of a hundred, and the one who does not reach the age of a hundred will be thought accursed. They will build houses and inhabit them; they will also plant vineyards and eat their fruit. They will not build and another inhabit, they will not plant and another eat; for as the lifetime of a tree, so will be the days of My people, and My chosen ones will fully enjoy the work of their hands. They will not labor in vain, or give birth to children for disaster; for they are the descendants of those blessed by the Lord, and their descendants with them. It will also come to pass that before they call, I will answer; while they are still speaking, I will listen. The wolf and the lamb will graze together, and the lion will eat straw like the ox; and dust will be the serpent's food. They will do no evil or harm on

all My holy mountain," says the Lord. (Isa. 65:17–25)

The final punctuation on this new creation is in chapter 66.

"For just as the new heavens and the new earth, which I make, will endure before Me," declares the Lord, "so will your descendants and your name endure. And it shall be from new moon to new moon and from Sabbath to Sabbath, all mankind will come to bow down before Me," says the Lord. (Isa. 66:22–23)

> *Anyone who followed Scripture was well–acquainted with the promises God had made His chosen people.*

There are a great many more mentions of the Lord's future kingdom in the rest of the prophetic books, but in order not to become tedious, the remainder of this chapter is in the Appendix along with sections relating to the kingdom written by the other prophets. You can read them there at your leisure. The point is made. Anyone who followed Scripture was well–acquainted with the promises God had made His chosen people.

QUESTIONS

1. What did God promise Abraham?

2. How did the life of Joseph represent both a dead and a returning Messiah?

3. What did God promise to David?

4. What is a main theme found in virtually all the prophetic books?

5. From which tribe is the ultimate king of Israel expected to come?

6. In which town would this king be born?

7.   What is prophesied about the future of Israel?

8.   In what city is the ultimate king predicted to reign?

The Parable of Wineskins

In the next few chapters, we will be covering the ways Jesus affirmed and identified with his Judaic faith in his ministry. The one occasion when Jesus did this most strikingly was in one of his parables—the parable of the wineskins. Unfortunately, this parable is frequently misunderstood. We will discuss the content and context of this parable, how it's commonly understood, and why it can't possibly have that meaning. Then we will explore what Jesus probably meant by it.

The event in question was narrated in each of the three synoptic Gospels: Matthew, Mark, and Luke. The account in Luke is the most complete since it includes some clarifying material to help us understand it better. For this reason, we will base our observations on that account.

And they said to Him, "The disciples of John often fast and offer prayers, the disciples of the Pharisees also do the same, but Yours eat and drink." And Jesus said to them, "You cannot make the attendants of the groom fast while the groom is with them, can you? But the days will come; and when the groom is taken away from them, then they will fast in those days." And He was also telling them a parable: "No one tears a piece of cloth from a new garment and puts it on an old garment; otherwise he will both tear the new, and the patch from the new garment will not match the old. And no one pours new wine into old wineskins; otherwise the new wine will burst the skins and it will be spilled out, and the skins will be ruined. But new wine must be put into fresh wineskins. And no one, after drinking old wine wants new; for he says, 'The old is fine.'" (Luke 5:33–39)

This explanation by Jesus is really more of a metaphor than a parable, in that it doesn't tell a story, but makes a comparison. Actually, it's a double metaphor in that two different scenarios are given of parallel circumstances that are obviously trying to teach the same lesson. Another structural feature to observe is that Jesus makes three statements that are grammatically parallel, "No one does such and such." This parallelism is even more evident in the Greek original, and it helps us to understand what Jesus is saying.

This metaphor is commonly understood to mean that Jesus' message is the new wine. Since it's new wine, it needs new wineskins (new structures) to accommodate it. It can't fit into the old wineskins of Judaism. When I was in college, I read a book entitled, *The Problem of Wineskins*, based on this understanding of the parable. It made a lot of sense to me at the time, and this is apparently how most interpreters understand this passage today.

Unfortunately, this cannot possibly be what Jesus had in mind when he spoke these words. Our biggest clue is that it's a double metaphor: Metaphor A is the garment and the patch and Metaphor B is the wine and the wineskins. It might be feasible to accept this understanding regarding the wineskin metaphor, but it's impossible to accept it for the garment and patch metaphor, which, incidentally, is the first of the two presented. If Jesus' message is that the new wine needs to be put in new wineskins, the equivalent lesson is that the new patch needs to be saved and used to patch a new garment. That's ridiculous! New garments don't need patching. If that's the meaning of the metaphor, it would make no sense. Unfortunately, many of us are so wedded to the idea that the message of Jesus was new that we're unable to consider alternate explanations.

Jesus knew as well as anybody that new things were usually better than old ones. If you're going to choose between a new car and an old one, all things being equal, you would choose the new one. But Jesus intentionally gave us a couple of exceptional situations, in which the new was not the best option for the task at hand, and even inferior in general.

If we paraphrased the first two statements Jesus made, they would amount to this: "No one patches an old garment with a new patch—the new patch will shrink and tear the garment. And no one fills an old wineskin with new wine—the wine will expand during the fermentation process and tear the wineskin."

> *It is not like the new patch that would rip the garment if used and it is not like the new wine that would destroy the wineskin.*

In both cases the new is presented as destructive in relation to the old. Jesus is not suggesting that his message destroys things. The parable makes much more sense if we see it as him explaining what his message is not. It is *not* like the new patch that would rip the garment if used and it is *not* like the new wine that would destroy the wineskin.

Just in case we still hadn't grasped his meaning, Jesus added a third parallel statement: "And no one, after drinking old wine wants new; for he says, 'The old is fine'" (Luke 5:39). Not only is the new presented as destructive, but in the case of wine the new is also *inferior* to the old. It seems very likely that Jesus was identifying his message with the old wine, or with an old patch that would be appropriate to use to repair a garment.

A primary reason this parable has been misinterpreted is that we don't understand Jesus' question. He begins with a coat that needs patching. The question is, "What do we patch it with?" The answer is, "Not a new patch because that won't work!" The implied answer is to find a patch that has been appropriately aged, so it will not damage the garment. Then he goes to an old wineskin. The question is, "What do we fill it with?" The answer is, "Not with new wine!" Once again, the implied answer is that it be filled with old wine which has already finished the fermentation process, so it will not burst the skins.

To understand what Jesus was getting at with this metaphor, it helps to step back and see what he might have been responding to at the time. There is not a lot of context given, but this parable seems to be connected to the question he was asked about why his disciples were not fasting when John's disciples and the disciples of other rabbis were fasting. There is an implied question behind this query: "Are you teaching something different than the other rabbis? Something new?" *New* is the key word to which Jesus seems to be responding.

Although this question is unstated in Luke's account, it had been verbalized in response to Jesus already. In Mark 1, when Jesus was in Capernaum, where he was when sharing this parable, people responded to a miraculous exorcism.

And Jesus rebuked him, saying, "Be silenced, and come forth out of him," and the unclean spirit having torn him, and having cried with a great voice, came forth out of him, and they were all amazed, so as to reason among themselves, saying, "What is this? what new teaching [is] this? that with authority also the unclean spirits he commandeth, and they obey him!" (Mark 1:25–27 YLT)

It's not so far-fetched to conjecture that this is the real question behind the Jewish leader's inquiry about Jesus' disciples fasting. Jesus responded as if the implied question was whether his message was something new. He explained that it was not a new teaching at all, but a unique circumstance: the presence of the Bridegroom. That's what accounted for the fact that his disciples aren't fasting. After the Bridegroom is gone, he says, his disciples will fast like everyone else. So nothing new, but something fulfilled instead.

He continued in this mode by illustrating how harmful it would be if he were actually bringing a new teaching. The old garment and the old wineskin represented the Judaism of his day. It may have been worn out and in need of repair, but it was still based on God's revelation through Moses and the prophets. If Jesus were bringing a message that was completely new, it would have been destructive to the very faith God had established since the beginning of time.

In reality, Jesus was saying the exact opposite of the common understanding of this passage in the church today. Jesus was emphatically declaring that his message was *not new*. It was the same Judaism the other rabbis were teaching. The difference was that he identified himself as the promised Davidic ruler of the ultimate kingdom of Israel, the King Messiah. He was the Bridegroom that was still with them, but would be taken away.

The parallelism inherent in Jesus' three statements is important because it connects their meaning. Those that interpret the parable in the common way are forced to break that parallelism. They claim that Jesus is saying that no one patches new *on* old or fills new *in* old because it would be foolish and counterproductive, but later, they're forced to admit that when Jesus said no one prefers new wine, he was saying they *should* because it is better. In this case, he's telling them they have poor judgment. It's not a parallel statement at all. This is yet another clue that Jesus is not saying what so many people think.

Here is an expanded paraphrase of what Jesus was saying, filling in some of the gaps:

"You people are asking if my message is new, something different than the Scriptures that the rabbis have been expounding. My answer is an unequivocal *no*! My message is based on the Scriptures of Judaism, plain and simple—just like theirs are. It's true that my disciples don't fast every time that the disciples of the Pharisees do. The reason for that is not a new message though. It's a unique circumstance. The Bridegroom is present, so they don't fast. When the Bridegroom is gone, they will fast.

"Imagine how damaging it would be to our biblical faith if I were teaching something completely new. If you need to patch the old coat of Judaism, you certainly wouldn't do it with a new patch. That would cause all kinds of problems. If you need to fill the old wineskin of Judaism, you certainly wouldn't fill it with new unfermented wine. That would be really destructive. And, after all, everybody agrees that old wine is better.

"If my message were actually something brand new, some new religion, in contrast to Judaism, it wouldn't take much to imagine my followers persecuting, and even killing, faithful Jews who are trying to follow the commands of God given through Moses. That's the kind of damage it could do if I were actually teaching something brand new.

"As you know, the prophets taught that in the last days, God would bring

Israel back from exile and establish the ultimate kingdom of Israel under King Messiah. I'm telling you that all that is true, and that I am King Messiah. If the nation will repent and turn back to God's commands, and accept me as the promised King, then the kingdom is at hand. If not, then we'll have to see what happens. The kingdom may be delayed for centuries. No matter what, God has promised that eventually it will come. That is my message to you."

QUESTIONS

1. In which chapter of Luke is the parable of wineskins most fully told?

2. What metaphor did Jesus use before mentioning wine and wineskins?

3. Why is a new patch not placed on an old garment?

4. What type patch is used to mend a new garment?

5. Assuming that Jesus' message is new, how is this metaphor commonly interpreted?

6. Why does that interpretation not work with the garment metaphor?

7. Why did Luke include the statement about old wine being preferred by everybody?

8. How is this statement parallel to Jesus' two previous statements?

9. What implied question is Jesus responding to when he tells this parable?

10. What is Jesus really claiming if all three of his statements are parallel?

CHAPTER 6

Jesus' Message

In some texts about Jesus' ministry, the word "gospel" is connected with his message. Before we consider what he meant by that term, let's give some thought to what his hearers would have thought in response to that concept.

The word "gospel" or "good news" is mentioned several times in the Old Testament. We know this because the same Greek word translated as "gospel" in the New Testament also commonly occurs in the Septuagint, the Greek version of the Old Testament that was written between the third and first centuries by Jewish scholars in Alexandria.

Several uses of this word and its related verbal forms are irrelevant for our purposes. For instance, it is used repeatedly of people bringing the news of Absalom's death to David, after Absalom and his followers revolted against David. However, David didn't consider it good news. David loved Absalom regardless of his foolish choices.

More relevant to our purposes is the use of this word by the prophets, especially Isaiah, who used it in four different contexts, one of which is partially quoted in Nahum 1:15. Probably the best-known is in Isaiah 52:

Therefore, My people shall know My name; therefore on that day I am the one who is speaking, "Here I am." How delightful on the mountains are the feet of one who brings good news, who announces peace and brings good news of happiness, who announces salvation, and says to Zion, "Your God reigns!" Listen! Your watchmen raise their voices, they shout joyfully together; for they will see with their own eyes when the Lord restores Zion. Be cheerful, shout joyfully together, you ruins of Jerusalem; for the Lord has comforted His people, He has redeemed Jerusalem. The Lord has bared His holy arm in the sight of all the nations, so that all the ends of the earth may see the salvation of our God. (Isa. 52:6–10)

This passage prophesies of the promised kingdom when God will gather His people back to Jerusalem and reign over them in the person of His Messiah. This event would definitely qualify as good news for all Israel.

Another passage in which Isaiah uses this word is in chapter 60:

Arise, shine; for thy light is come, and the glory of the Lord is risen upon thee. For, behold, the darkness shall cover the earth, and gross darkness the people: but the Lord shall arise upon thee, and his glory shall be seen upon thee. And the Gentiles shall come to thy light, and kings to the brightness of thy rising. Lift up thine eyes round about, and see: all they gather themselves together, they come to thee: thy sons shall come from far, and thy daughters shall be nursed at thy side. Then thou shalt see, and flow together, and thine heart shall fear, and be enlarged; because the abundance of the sea shall be converted unto thee, the forces of the Gentiles shall come unto thee. The multitude of camels shall cover thee, the dromedaries of Midian and Ephah; all they from Sheba shall come: they shall bring gold and incense; and they shall shew forth the praises of the Lord. (Isa. 60:1–6 KJV)

The word translated "shew forth" in verse 6 is the verbal form of the "gospel," meaning to proclaim good news. The previous context establishes that Isaiah was writing about a time of peace and prosperity that will accompany this future kingdom, and it's notable that this kingdom was inclusive of everyone in the world. All people! The rest of the chapter elaborates on the good things that will happen to Israel as a result of that kingdom.

In Isaiah 61, Isaiah used the same word again in the passage that Jesus quoted when speaking in the synagogue in Nazareth.[1]

The Spirit of the Lord God is upon me, because the Lord anointed me to bring good news to the humble; He has sent me to bind up the brokenhearted, to proclaim release to captives and freedom to prisoners; to proclaim the favorable year of the Lord and the day of vengeance of our God; to comfort all who mourn, to grant those who mourn in Zion, giving them a garland instead of ashes, the oil of gladness instead of mourning, the cloak of praise instead of a disheartened spirit. So they will be called oaks of righteousness, the planting of the Lord, that He may be glorified. (Isa. 61:1–3)

The context of these sections in Isaiah are obvious descriptions of the manifest kingdom of God. When Jesus read from this passage, he finished with, "This day is this scripture fulfilled in your ears" (Luke 4:21 KJV).

The last of the four passages in Isaiah that reference the good news is not so obvious, but it's still informative to examine it.

Go up on a high mountain, Zion, messenger of good news, raise your voice forcefully, Jerusalem, messenger of good news; raise it up, do not fear. Say to the cities of Judah, "Here is your God!" Behold, the Lord God will come with

---
1 See Luke 4:16–21.

might, with His arm ruling for Him. Behold, His compensation is with Him, and His reward before Him. Like a shepherd He will tend His flock, in His arm He will gather the lambs and carry them in the fold of His robe; He will gently lead the nursing ewes. (Isa. 40:9–11)

This good news is the coming and ruling of God, with its accompanying rewards, but with special attention to the gentle tending of his flock, which is compared to the way a shepherd cares for his sheep. Therefore, this passage also relates to the coming kingdom.

When Jesus' followers heard the word "gospel," they would have naturally associated it with the coming of this promised kingdom.

All of these passages would have been familiar to Jesus' hearers. When Jesus' followers heard the word "gospel," they would have naturally associated it with the coming of this promised kingdom. There's no question that this is the thrust of Jesus' message for most of his ministry.

Jesus associated the word "gospel" with his message over a dozen times. He didn't always explicitly call it "the gospel of the kingdom," but he definitely did on four occasions: three in Matthew and one in Mark. The other times he referred to the gospel, we are left to infer that he was referring to the kingdom.

A characteristic passage describing Jesus' early message is found in Matthew 4:

Jesus was going about in all of Galilee, teaching in their synagogues and proclaiming the gospel of the kingdom, and healing every disease and every sickness among the people. And the news about Him spread throughout Syria; and they brought to Him all who were ill, those suffering with various diseases and severe pain, demon–possessed, people with epilepsy, and people who were paralyzed; and He healed them. Large crowds followed Him from Galilee and the Decapolis, and Jerusalem, and Judea, and from beyond the Jordan. (Matt. 4:23–25)

His message of good news attracted large crowds. Similar passages are found in Matthew 9:35 and Mark 1:14–15.

When Jesus first declared his message, it matched the message of his cousin, John: "Repent ye: for the kingdom of heaven is at hand" (Matt. 3:2 KJV). John often elaborated on what this repentance looked like for different kinds of people. It involved turning back to God's commands that He had given Moses. Many of the promises involving the kingdom were conditional on the people's obedience to those commands. When people expressed their repentance and their intention to live obediently, John immersed them in water, usually in the Jordan River. Immersion was a common Jewish practice for purifying oneself before entering the temple courts.

Another key aspect of John's message is that, although the kingdom is near, John was not its king. In fact, he went to great lengths to point out that Jesus was the one whose greatness he was proclaiming.[2] John was declaring both the nearness of the kingdom and identifying the king.

Let's look, then, at how Jesus defined his message when he first began preaching. Examples are found most clearly in Matthew and Mark.

---

2 Compare Matthew 3:11–17; Mark 1:7–8; Luke 3:15–18; and John 1:19–27.

Matthew 4:17 in KJV says, "From that time Jesus began to preach, and to say, Repent: for the kingdom of heaven is at hand." This is identical to John the Baptist's message in Matthew 3:2, except that Jesus claims to be the king, while John does not.

In Mark's version, Jesus shares a similar message. "Now after John was taken into custody, Jesus came into Galilee, preaching the gospel of God, and saying, 'The time is fulfilled, and the kingdom of God is at hand; repent and believe in the gospel'" (Mark 1:14–15). The elements here are the same: the nearness of the kingdom and the need for repentance. Mark also emphasized the good news (gospel) aspect of this message, just as Matthew did in other passages.

It's interesting to note that Matthew referred to the "kingdom of heaven" while Mark and Luke called it the "kingdom of God." As we've seen in the prophets, the promised kingdom had nothing to do with what we think of as heaven. It was a kingdom on earth with Jerusalem as its capital. Why, then, did Matthew call it the "kingdom of heaven"?

As you may be aware, Jews, both then and now, were reluctant to pronounce the holy name of God because of the commandment against "taking the Lord's name in vain." The thinking goes that if you don't say the Name at all, you can't take it in vain, so a substitute word is typically used. In many cases they substituted the word "Lord," or its equivalent in Hebrew, *Adonai*. Many Bible translations put "LORD" in all capital letters to indicate that it was a substitute for the name of God represented by the Hebrew letters *YHWH* or *YHVH*. These four letters are called the Tetragrammaton, and represent the name of God used in the Hebrew Bible.

The original pronunciation of the name has been lost, but many have tried to guess what it may have been. For most of its existence, the Hebrew text of the Bible consisted of only consonants. In the Middle Ages, the

Masoretes added vowel points to the text. However, to prevent people from trying to pronounce the Name, they placed the vowel points of the word *Adonai* with it, so that when people read it, they pronounced it as *Adonai*. This is actually the source of the "word" *Jehovah*. It was derived from God's name with the vowel points of *Adonai* added to it. It was never intended to be a word at all! This is verified by the fact that when the Name occurs alongside the Hebrew word *Adonai*, the Name is pointed with the vowels of *Elohim*, meaning "God." So if you tried to pronounce the result, it would come out something like "Jehovee." Again, Jehovah is not a word that even appears naturally in the Bible. It is simply the vowels of one word added to the consonants of another.

The Jews in the first century would not pronounce the name of God. There's no evidence that Jesus ever pronounced it either. For some, even using the word "God" as an appellation was borderline inappropriate. This is probably why Matthew used the word "heaven" as a substitute for "God." This was probably a common custom in those days when speaking of the kingdom. We don't know whether Matthew or Mark cited the actual term that Jesus used, but "kingdom of God" is its most literal meaning.

As previously mentioned, when Jesus first announced his message, he did it in a synagogue in his home town of Nazareth on the Sabbath, as was his custom. He read a passage from Isaiah 61 that clearly referred to the promised kingdom, and then claimed that the Scripture was now fulfilled. He was clear as crystal: he was the king and therefore, he was offering the kingdom.

And He came to Nazareth, where He had been brought up; and as was His custom, He entered the synagogue on the Sabbath, and stood up to read. And the scroll of Isaiah the prophet was handed to Him. And He unrolled the scroll and found the place where it was written: "The Spirit of the Lord is upon Me, because He anointed Me to bring good news to the poor. He has sent Me to proclaim release to captives, and recovery of sight to the blind, to set free those who are oppressed, to proclaim the favorable year of the Lord." And He rolled up the scroll, gave it back to the attendant, and sat down; and the eyes of all the people in the synagogue were intently directed at Him. Now He began to say to them, "Today this Scripture has been fulfilled in your hearing." (Luke 4:16–21)

A similar statement is made later: "And it came to pass afterward, that he went throughout every city and village, preaching and shewing the glad tidings of the kingdom of God" (Luke 8:1). Matthew and Mark also affirm that he preached this message in synagogues.

And Jesus went about all Galilee, teaching in their synagogues, and preaching the gospel of the kingdom, and healing all manner of sickness and all manner of disease among the people. (Matt. 4:23 KJV)

And they went into Capernaum; and straightway on the sabbath day he entered into the synagogue, and taught. (Mark 1:21 KJV)

The response to Jesus' fervent claim is telling. It makes it plain that his hearers understood what he was asserting, and they immediately rejected that claim. This happened:

And all the people in the synagogue were filled with rage as they heard these things; and they got up and drove Him out of the city, and brought Him to the crest of the hill on which their city had been built, so that they could throw Him down from the cliff. But He passed through their midst and went on His way. (Luke 4:28–30)

And Jesus didn't stop with them. He never wavered in making his identity plain to any that would listen. In all three of the synoptic Gospels, Jesus expressed the need to preach the same message elsewhere in the region. We've already seen the statements in Matthew 4:23 and Luke 8:1. Here are two more:

And he said unto them, I must preach the kingdom of God to other cities also: for therefore am I sent. And he preached in the synagogues of Galilee. (Luke 4:43–44 KJV)

And he said unto them, Let us go into the next towns, that I may preach there also: for therefore came I forth. And he preached in their synagogues throughout all Galilee, and cast out devils. (Mark 1:38–39 KJV)

Later in his ministry, when Jesus sent his disciples out to preach, he pointedly charged them with the same message. In Matthew 10, he told them, "And as ye go, preach, saying, the kingdom of heaven is at hand" (Matt. 10:7 KJV). The parallel passage in Mark reads, "And they went out, and preached that men should repent" (Mark 6:12 KJV). Luke puts it like this: "And he sent them to preach the kingdom of God, and to heal the sick" (Luke 9:2 KJV). Whether Jesus or his disciples were preaching, the message was the same: the kingdom of God was ready to be established with Jesus as King if people would repent.

After John was put in prison, he grew discouraged, and began doubting whether Jesus really was the King he claimed to be. John sent his disciples to ask Jesus if he was really the Messiah, or if that person was still coming. Jesus' response to him was a sure affirmation that the kingdom really was being offered and that Jesus had the authority to do that.

Now while in prison, John heard about the works of Christ, and he sent word by his disciples, and said to Him, "Are You the Coming One, or are we to look for someone else?" Jesus answered and said to them, "Go and report to John what you hear and see: those who are blind receive sight and those who limp walk, those with leprosy are cleansed and those who are deaf hear, the dead are raised, and the poor have the gospel preached to them. And blessed is any person who does not take offense at Me." (Matt. 11:2–6)

The evidence Jesus gave matched what the prophets had promised in passages like the one he had chosen to read when he first began preaching in the synagogue in his home town: Isaiah 61.

Most of the specifics of Jesus' message are found in the synoptic Gospels, but the Gospel of John is not silent about this message either. In John 2, Jesus performed a miracle at a wedding in Cana. He created an abundant amount of excellent wine from stone pots of water. This abundance of old wine reflected various prophecies[3] of the prosperity in the promised kingdom.

Now the Lord of armies will prepare a lavish banquet for all peoples on this mountain; a banquet of aged wine, choice pieces with marrow, and refined, aged wine. (Isa. 25:6)

Hear the word of the Lord, O ye nations, and declare it in the isles afar off, and say, He that scattered Israel will gather him, and keep him, as a shepherd doth his flock. For the Lord hath redeemed Jacob, and ransomed him from the hand of him that was stronger than he. Therefore they shall come and sing in the height of Zion, and shall flow together to the goodness of the Lord, for

3 Examples can be found in Isaiah 55:1–5; Joel 2:19, 24; 3:18; and Amos 9:13 in addition to these.

wheat, and for wine, and for oil, and for the young of the flock and of the herd: and their soul shall be as a watered garden; and they shall not sorrow any more at all. (Jeremiah 31:10–12 KJV)

Also found in John is the clear statement by Jesus that he is the Messiah, which he made when speaking to the Samaritan woman at the well.

The woman said to Him, "I know that Messiah is coming (He who is called Christ); when that One comes, He will declare all things to us." Jesus said to her, "I am He, the One speaking to you." (John 4:25–26)

This matches up with many other testimonies at the time.[4]

When Jesus taught his disciples to pray, he told them to pray for the coming of the kingdom. "Pray, then, in this way: Our Father, who is in heaven, hallowed be Your name. Your kingdom come" (Matt. 6:9–10). This is significant as it mirrors the passage in which Isaiah urged people to pray for the coming of the kingdom. "You who profess the Lord, take no rest for yourselves; and give Him no rest until He establishes and makes Jerusalem an object of praise on the earth" (Isa. 62:6b–7).

When Jesus told parables, especially in Matthew 13, he often began them with the phrase, "The kingdom of heaven is like...." Several lessons are taught through these "kingdom" parables—primarily that the kingdom starts very small and grows larger and larger; involves separating the righteous from the unrighteous, and is worth sacrificing everything to attain. In fact, elsewhere Jesus urged his listeners to make the kingdom their highest priority. "But seek first His kingdom and His righteousness, and all these things will be provided to you" (Matt. 6:33).

4 See Matthew 16:16; Mark 8:29; Luke 9:20; and John 1:41.

The repentance Jesus entwined in his kingdom message was a call to return to the commands of God given through Moses. Jesus stated that two commands are the heart of Torah, and sum up all the others: the command to love God found in Deuteronomy 6:5 and the command to love one's neighbor found in Leviticus 19:18. Much of Jesus' teaching on love is a response to questions about how to carry out this command to love one's neighbor. However, all this teaching is ultimately connected to his plea to repent, so that the kingdom the prophets promised could be realized.

All of this preaching about repentance and the arrival of the kingdom was at the heart of Judaism—then and now. It reflects the hope of Jews everywhere: that God will regather his people from exile and anoint a descendant of David to rule over them in an era of peace and plenty when people will automatically follow God's commands because they are internally motivated to do so.

It's true that later in his ministry, when it became clear that the Jewish leaders were set on opposing Jesus' claims, his message shifted, and he began announcing his imminent suffering and death as a payment for sin. That message is also totally Jewish. It is the very heart of Isaiah's description of the servant of the Lord. The point is that Jesus' entire message was consistent with the teaching of the Hebrew Scripture that was given through Moses and the prophets.

QUESTIONS

1. What does Jesus mean when he refers to the gospel of the kingdom?

2. What expression of Jesus' message is the same as that proclaimed by his relative, John the Baptist?

3. What was the difference between Jesus' message and John's?

4. How do Matthew and Luke refer to the kingdom differently?

5. Why does Matthew refer to it as the kingdom of "heaven"?

6. After John was put in prison, what question did he ask Jesus?

7. How did Jesus respond?

8. How did Jesus instruct his disciples to pray regarding the kingdom?

9. What lessons do Jesus' parables about the kingdom of heaven teach?

10. What two commands did Jesus say are the most important and sum up the entire Law?

11. What is the hope of Judaism—then and now?

CHAPTER 7

Affirmations of Judaism

Many times during his ministry, Jesus said or did something that affirmed the fact that his convictions corresponded to his faith in Judaism. Jesus adhered to the Law of God given through Moses in all his actions, and directed others to do the same. We will only be able to look at a small sampling of these affirmations of Judaism, but there are many.

One of the strongest and most unequivocal is contained in the parable of the rich man and Lazarus in Luke 16. As you'll recall, Jesus told the story of a nameless rich man and a poor beggar named Lazarus who both died. The rich man's spirit ended up in Gehenna, the place of torment, while Lazarus was taken by angels to the lap of Abraham in paradise. At some point, the rich man begs Abraham to send Lazarus to talk to his five brothers, so they won't also end up in a place of torment.

And he said, "Then I request of you, father, that you send him to my father's house—for I have five brothers—in order that he may warn them, so that they will not come to this place of torment as well." But Abraham said, "They

have Moses and the Prophets; let them hear them." But he said, "No, father
Abraham, but if someone goes to them from the dead, they will repent!"'But he
said to him, "If they do not listen to Moses and the Prophets, they will not be
persuaded even if someone rises from the dead." (Luke 16:27–31)

This is quite a statement! Jesus was maintaining that Moses and the
prophets and the Hebrew Bible contained *all that was necessary* to learn
how to avoid this place of torment after death. This should give us food for
thought. The Bible is clear that anyone who avoids the place of torment
does so by the grace of God. For Jesus to claim that Moses and the prophets
are a stronger source of guidance than someone rising from the dead, as
Jesus himself would do in the coming days, is an amazing statement. He is
strongly affirming the power of the biblical teachings of Judaism.

A similar statement is found in the Sermon on the Mount in Matthew
5. Jesus was teaching large crowds as well as the Twelve. Jesus said to them:

Think not that I am come to destroy the law, or the prophets: I am not come to
destroy, but to fulfil. For verily I say unto you, till heaven and earth pass, one
jot or one tittle shall in no wise pass from the law, till all be fulfilled. Whosoever
therefore shall break one of these least commandments, and shall teach men
so, he shall be called the least in the kingdom of heaven: but whosoever shall
do and teach them, the same shall be called great in the kingdom of heaven.
(Matt. 5:17–19 KJV)

Jesus must have foreseen that the idea would eventually arise among his
followers that he had abolished the Law of Moses. This statement was a
strong repudiation of that conclusion. Some may have thought that the
Law would be abolished when Jesus died, just a few months in the future.
But the time frame Jesus referred to was "till heaven and earth pass." We
also need to note that the last phrase of verse 18, "till all be fulfilled," doesn't

use the Greek word that refers to prophecy being fulfilled, but the one that means "until everything happens." It's clear from Jesus' statement that if the Law was ever to be abolished, it wouldn't happen until at least the end of the messianic kingdom era when a new heaven and new earth had been established.

...if the Law was ever to be abolished, it wouldn't happen until at least the end of the messianic kingdom era when a new heaven and new earth had been established.

We've seen plenty of verses in the writings of the prophets that indicated that the Law would be the standard of behavior in the ultimate kingdom of Israel. In fact, it said that the Law would be internalized and enforced through the working of the Spirit of God.[1] Jesus strongly affirmed the continuity of the Law. He even went on to say that those who practiced and taught these commands would be called great in the kingdom. There is not any ambiguity about his statement whatsoever.

Incidentally, the Hebrew Scriptures, called the Old Testament by Christians, are known by Jews according to the three sections into which they are divided: the Law (Torah), the Prophets, and the Writings. Sometimes it's shortened to Torah and the Prophets, and other times, it's called the Law, the Prophets, and the Psalms, as the Book of Psalms is the first book of the collection of the Writings. What we might think of as historical books are considered the Former Prophets, and the writings of the post–exilic prophets are considered the Latter Prophets, sometimes

---

1 See Jeremiah 31:33 and Ezekiel 36:27.

called the Major and Minor Prophets in Christian circles today. However, there is nothing "minor" about the Minor Prophets. Whenever Jesus or one of his followers referred to these, they were talking about this entire body of Scriptures. These were the only ones they had at that point.

While we're discussing the Sermon on the Mount, we might also take note of an element of Jewish tradition that was active in the first century and passed down orally by the rabbis until it was written down a few centuries later. One collection of these oral traditions is a document called *Pirkei Avot* (Chapters of the Fathers). It begins by saying, "Moses received the Torah from Sinai and handed it down to Joshua; Joshua to the Elders; the Elders to the Prophets; the Prophets handed it down to the Men of the Great Assembly. The latter said three things: Be cautious in judgment, raise up many disciples, and make a fence for the Law." This idea of making a "fence" around the Torah involved setting standards of behavior that would prevent a person from getting into a situation in which they would be tempted to break the Law. An example of this might be for a married man to avoid being alone with a woman who isn't his wife in order to avoid temptation to sin.

This "building a fence" around the Law was exactly what Jesus did in the Sermon on the Mount. He often reflected a commandment, or the understanding of a commandment, by saying, "You have heard it said...." Right afterward though, Jesus would build a fence by saying, "But I say to you...." This was followed by a standard that was even more rigid to prevent being tempted to break the commandment.

For I say to you that unless your righteousness far surpasses that of the scribes and Pharisees, you will not enter the kingdom of heaven. You have heard that the ancients were told, "You shall not murder," and "Whoever commits murder shall be answerable to the court." But I say to you that everyone who is angry with his brother shall be answerable to the court; and whoever says to his brother, "You good–for–nothing," shall be answerable to the supreme court; and whoever says, "You fool," shall be guilty enough to go into the fiery hell...You have heard that it was said, 'You shall not commit adultery'; but I say to you that everyone who looks at a woman with lust for her has already committed adultery with her in his heart.... Again, you have heard that the ancients were told, "You shall not make false vows, but shall fulfill your vows to the Lord." But I say to you, take no oath at all, neither by heaven, for it is the throne of God, nor by the earth, for it is the footstool of His feet, nor by Jerusalem, for it is the city of the great King. Nor shall you take an oath by your head, for you cannot make a single hair white or black. But make sure your statement is, "Yes, yes" or "No, no"; anything beyond these is of evil origin.... You have heard that it was said, 'You shall love your neighbor and hate your enemy.' But I say to you, love your enemies and pray for those who persecute you, so that you may prove yourselves to be sons of your Father who is in heaven; for He causes His sun to rise on the evil and the good, and sends rain on the righteous and the unrighteous. (Matt. 5:21–22, 27–28, 33–37, 43–45)

So Jesus' approach was exactly what the rabbis referred to as building a fence around the Law, implicitly affirming their teaching in this area. Another affirmation of Judaism in the teaching of Jesus is in John 4. Jesus was talking with a Samaritan woman at the well in Sychar. Shortly before he told her that he was the promised Messiah, we read this exchange:

The woman said to Him, "Sir, I perceive that You are a prophet. Our fathers worshiped on this mountain, and yet you Jews say that in Jerusalem is the place where one must worship." Jesus said to her, "Believe Me, woman, that a time is coming when you will worship the Father neither on this mountain nor in Jerusalem. You Samaritans worship what you do not know; we worship what we do know, because salvation is from the Jews." (John 4:19–22)

Another amazing statement by Jesus! "Salvation is from the Jews." Christians, when considering this phrase, seem to think that it only points to the fact that Jesus was ethnically a Jew, but it goes much deeper than that. Jesus is contrasting the beliefs of the Samaritans with the beliefs of the Jews—especially with regard to the place and means of properly worshiping God. He clearly stands on the side of the Jews. We can debate about exactly what he meant by "salvation" in this passage, but he credits the idea to the teaching and Scripture of the Jews. Another affirmation of Judaism and the Jewish Scriptures!

Most Christians are aware of the criticisms Jesus levied over the teachers of the Law and the Pharisees in Matthew 23, but are much less familiar with the statement Jesus made at the beginning of that passage:

Then Jesus spoke to the crowds and to His disciples, saying: "The scribes and the Pharisees have seated themselves in the chair of Moses. Therefore, whatever they tell you, do and comply with it all, but do not do as they do; for they say things and do not do them. (Matt. 23:1–3).

Jesus made it clear that it was *not the teaching* of the Pharisees he was criticizing, but their hypocrisy. There is nothing wrong with the Law. The Pharisees were teaching correctly, but they were not doing what they taught. In fact, the teachings of Jesus line up with the teachings of the Pharisees more than any other Jewish sect of the day. It's a common idea that Jesus didn't want to adhere to the Law as strictly as the Pharisees did, but in actual fact, Jesus criticized the actions of the Pharisees more than once in not keeping the Law strictly enough.[2] As we just read in Matthew 5, the standard of Torah–observance that Jesus recommended *exceeded* that of the Pharisees and teachers of the Law, but he did affirm their teaching and instructed his hearers to obey them, thus affirming Judaism once again.

Another thing that we need to notice is that when Jesus healed a man with leprosy, he ordered him to go to the temple and show himself to the priest and follow the procedure to be readmitted to the temple in Leviticus 14.

And a man with leprosy came to Him and bowed down before Him, and said, "Lord, if You are willing, You can make me clean." Jesus reached out with His hand and touched him, saying, "I am willing; be cleansed." And immediately his leprosy was cleansed. And Jesus said to him, "See that you tell no one; but go, show yourself to the priest and present the offering that Moses commanded, as a testimony to them." (Matt. 8:2–4)

This story is also recorded in Luke 5:12–14. It's notable that Jesus insisted that the procedures laid out in the Law be followed to the smallest detail. A similar affirmation is found in the story of Jesus' temptation by the Devil at the beginning of his ministry. This event is mentioned in all three synoptic Gospels, but Matthew and Luke give the most detailed account. In both of these, Jesus was presented with three different temptations, and each time he responded by citing a passage from the book of Deuteronomy. This showed that not only did Jesus know the books of the Law very well, but that he used them as his guide for living.[3]

It's worth noting that Jesus invariably attended the local synagogue

---

2 See Matthew 23:23 and Mark 7:9–13.

3 See Matthew 4:1–11 and Luke 4:1–13.

on the Sabbath wherever he happened to be. There are a dozen or more verses that recount his visiting and speaking in various synagogues on the Sabbath. Luke 4:16 states explicitly that it was his custom to attend the synagogue on the Sabbath.

Jesus also traveled to Jerusalem for the biblical feast days, as commanded in Deuteronomy 16:16 (KJV): "Three times in a year shall all thy males appear before the Lord thy God in the place which he shall choose; in the feast of unleavened bread, and in the feast of weeks, and in the feast of tabernacles." Most of these visits are recorded in the Gospel of John in which there are at least two mentions of him going to Jerusalem for Passover,[4] once for Tabernacles,[5] and once for an unnamed feast.[6] Since Jesus lived in Galilee most of the time, this meant he walked ninety miles to fulfill his temple worship according to Torah, but he was a follower of God's commands and so he went.

As we've seen, Jesus' entire lifestyle was devoted to practicing and affirming the guidance given by God in the Law of Moses. This is a clear affirmation of Judaism. The closer we look, the clearer it becomes that Jesus taught and lived according to the teachings of Judaism and the Hebrew Scriptures.

---

4 See John 2:13 and 12:12.
5 See John 7:2–10.
6 See John 5:1.

QUESTIONS

---

1. What did Jesus say in his parable of the rich man and Lazarus that affirmed his Judaism?

2. In Matthew 5, what did Jesus claim would not happen until heaven and earth passed away?

3. What will characterize those who will be called great in the kingdom?

4. What three sections of the Bible compose the Hebrew Scriptures?

5. How did Jesus demonstrate the idea of "making a fence" around Torah in his Sermon on the Mount?

6.   When speaking with the woman at the well in John 4, who did Jesus say was the source of salvation?

7.   Before Jesus criticized the hypocrisy of some Pharisees in Matthew 23, what did he say to affirm their teaching?

8.   What did Jesus tell the man healed of leprosy to do?

9.   When Jesus was tempted by the Devil, what book did he quote in response?

10.   What was the custom of Jesus to do on the Sabbath?

11.   Why did Jesus go to Jerusalem one or more times every year?

CHAPTER 8

Controversies

People come up with various reasons for rejecting the idea that Jesus taught Judaism. We will discuss some of the objections in this chapter.

One objection is based on a passage in Mark 7.

And He said to them, "Are you so lacking in understanding as well? Do you not understand that whatever goes into the person from outside cannot defile him, because it does not go into his heart, but into his stomach, and is eliminated?" (Thereby He declared all foods clean.) And He was saying, "That which comes out of the person, that is what defiles the person. For from within, out of the hearts of people, come the evil thoughts, acts of sexual immorality, thefts, murders, acts of adultery, deeds of greed, wickedness, deceit, indecent behavior, envy, slander, pride, and foolishness. All these evil things come from within and defile the person." (Mark 7:18–23)

Some translations render the last part of verse 19 to say, "In saying this, Jesus declared all foods 'clean.'" This is one of several instances in which the translators, knowing that their primary market was Gentile Christians, apparently "translated" it in a way they thought that group would want it to read. In reality, the original Greek text says nothing like that, and it's quite the stretch to understand it that way. The context also strongly gravitates against that meaning.

Mark 7 begins with some Pharisees and teachers of the Law objecting to Jesus' disciples eating food without performing a ritual handwashing based on their traditions. Jesus responded by pointing out that this tradition they adhered to so closely had no basis in Scripture. It had been initiated by men from the onset. In contrast, they were avoiding keeping one of the commands God had announced from Mount Sinai: the command to honor one's parents. They had circumvented this command by allowing people to pledge the money that should have been used to support their parents as a gift to the temple instead. Jesus vigorously renounced the substitution of man–made traditions for the commands in the Law. That's the context here, so it is unthinkable that a few seconds later, he would suddenly renounce the food laws that he himself followed, thereby canceling some of God's commands—the very issue he just brought up with the Pharisees.

Jesus went on to explain that it was not what went into your body (food) that led a person to sin, but what came out of the heart. It is at this point that the phrase in question appears: "In saying this, Jesus declared all foods 'clean.'" Translated literally, the phrase would read, "purging all foods." The King James does much better by translating it "purging all meats" which is closer. The most natural understanding is that it is the exiting from the body that purges all foods. They are no longer part of your system, so no longer have any effect on you at all.

Instead, some interpreters choose to understand it as a parenthetical statement thrown in by the author of the Gospel to interpret Jesus' words. The problem with that is that not only do you have to go back two full verses to connect the two, but nothing Jesus said in this conversation could be taken to indicate this concept. God had prohibited some items, like pork and shellfish, from being eaten by His people.[1] Those were not considered food, and would not have been described using the word for food.

There is another reason why it is virtually impossible to understand this passage as Jesus negating the commands of God as later related in Acts 10. In Acts 10, Peter, who had been with Jesus during his entire ministry and had heard all his preaching, had a vision of a sheet descending with all kinds of animals in it. Peter heard a voice telling him to kill and eat. Three times Peter refused because he followed the dietary laws that God gave. If Jesus had ever taught, or even hinted, that the dietary laws, or any of God's commands, were no longer in effect, Peter's actions would have been very different. Peter concluded that the vision was ultimately about people, not animals.[2] He should be commended for standing firm for God's commands, even when an unknown voice was telling him to break those commands. The point is that Peter still held a strict perspective regarding adhering to the Law God gave through Moses, even after listening to *all* of Jesus' preaching and teaching. It seems fair to conclude that Jesus taught obedience to that Law, especially since he stated that plainly throughout his ministry.[3]

It's worth noting that nowhere in the Gospels do we have any record of Jesus eating anything prohibited in the Torah, or teaching that this was permissible. He even told a parable that involved separating good fish from the bad in Matthew 13:48. This assumes that some fish (those with fins and scales) were permissible to eat, while others weren't. It would have been totally contrary to Jesus' character and teaching to contradict God's laws.

---

1 See Deuteronomy 14 for these.

2 See Acts 10:17, 28.

3 See Matthew 5:17–19.

Another objection that is commonly raised is that Jesus "fulfilled the Law" so that it is no longer in effect. The statement that Jesus fulfilled the law is made in Matthew 5:17, but the next verses go on to say that not a jot or tittle will pass from the Law *until heaven and earth pass away*, and that whoever keeps the Law and teaches others to do the same will be called great in the kingdom. Obviously, heaven and earth had not yet passed away. Jesus' position on the *continuation* of the Law could not be clearer.

What, then, did Matthew mean when he wrote that Jesus came to fulfill the Law? The Law is not a prediction that someone "fulfills" by making it come true. It's a set of instructions that Jesus fulfilled by keeping each part in its entirety, *as no man had ever done before.* There is no reason in the world to assume that fulfilling the Mosaic Law would cause it to be canceled as God's instructions for living.

> *There is no reason in the world to assume that fulfilling the Mosaic Law would cause it to be canceled as God's instructions for living.*

Others point to passages like Matthew 11:13 that say that all the prophets and the Law prophesied until John. They assume that this means that something about them ceased after John. The statement does not imply that at all. For example, if a road goes to Omaha, that doesn't imply that it doesn't continue beyond it. The truth is that much of what the prophets taught about the final ingathering of Israel has not happened yet. It's also important to note that the phrase "the Law and the Prophets" was commonly used during Jesus' time to refer to the Hebrew Scriptures, all of which were written before John.

A similar passage is found in John. "For the law was given by Moses, but grace and truth came by Jesus Christ" (John 1:17 KJV). This passage is not implying that the Law of Moses did not involve grace or truth, or that Jesus opposed that Law. Rather, it is drawing a parallel. Moses was the greatest teacher of Judaism to that date. God gave His precious instructions for His chosen people through Moses, and Moses was revered as the ultimate prophet of all time. The point of the verse is that Jesus is on the level of Moses. It also leads us to the fact that Moses prophetically wrote about a future prophet that God would send—one who would be like him.[4] Jesus is that Prophet, but he is more than a prophet. Jesus claimed to have a special relationship with God and to be the king of the kingdom of Israel. John was pointing out that Moses brought good things, but Jesus brought even better things.

Others think Jesus broke the Mosaic Law when he healed people on the Sabbath. That is certainly the point that some of the teachers of the Law during that time were trying to make at several junctures in Jesus' ministry. We need to remember that although God commanded His people to remember the Sabbath day and keep it holy, and do all their work on the other six days, the actual requirements for the Sabbath are kind of vague. On occasion in the Law, God specified that certain things were not to be done, such as gathering manna or firewood or starting a fire, but for the most part, the specifics were left unstated.

In later years, rabbis put together a list of things that traditionally should not be done on the Sabbath, and these things may or may not be in line with what God intended when He gave that command. Jesus was not

---

4 See Deuteronomy 18:18–19.

breaking the Law when he healed on the Sabbath. His point is that his actions are not contrary to God's command at all, but that he understood God's intent better than some of the leaders did. Every time the teachers criticized him for healing on the Sabbath, his replies indicated that it was the right thing to do.

> *Departing from there, He went into their synagogue. And a man was there whose hand was withered. And they questioned Jesus, asking, "Is it lawful to heal on the Sabbath?"—so that they might bring charges against Him. But He said to them, "What man is there among you who has a sheep, and if it falls into a pit on the Sabbath, will he not take hold of it and lift it out? How much more valuable then is a person than a sheep! So then, it is lawful to do good on the Sabbath." (Matt. 12:9–12)*

> *Jesus said to them, "The Sabbath was made for man, and not man for the Sabbath." (Mark 2:27)*

Jesus' main point was that the Sabbath command was meant to be a blessing, not a burden. It wasn't so much a list of things to avoid as an opportunity to express love for God by dedicating a day to Him.

Many people also assume that Jesus was disregarding Law on the Sabbath when his disciples gathered grain on the Sabbath and Jesus defended them, as related in Matthew 12. Jesus responded with several counterexamples to show that sustaining life was a priority in interpreting God's commands. The Sabbath was an appropriate time for doing that as shown in the case of feeding hungry people and in healing sick people.

On a slightly different topic, another passage that people point to is in John 18:36 where Jesus says, "My kingdom is not of this world. If it were, my servants would fight to prevent my arrest by the Jews. But now my kingdom is from another place." They conclude that the kingdom Jesus spoke of is a "spiritual" kingdom, not a literal one. But Jesus is speaking of the source of his kingdom. By this time, the Jewish leaders had rejected Jesus' offer to establish this kingdom. It was clear this was not going to happen in his lifetime. Nevertheless, Jesus went on to insist that he was a king, though his kingdom was from another place. "Therefore Pilate said to Him, 'So You are a king?' Jesus answered, 'You say correctly that I am a king. For this purpose I have been born, and for this I have come into the world: to testify to the truth. Everyone who is of the truth listens to My voice'" (John 18:37). In context, Jesus was plainly talking about the kingdom the prophets wrote about, which would be a literal kingdom on the earth, and would now be delayed until a future time. It would not be a kingdom "of this world" but from God.

Another similar passage that people misunderstand is found in Luke 17:21, which says, "Nor will they say, 'Look, here it is!' or, 'There it is!' For behold, the kingdom of God is in your midst." Many translations render Jesus' words as, "The kingdom of God is within you," implying an internal rule of the heart, but the passage could just as easily be translated as the NASB does with "in your midst," which would reflect Jesus' presence with them representing the kingdom which Jesus said was "at hand." This is a much more consistent way to understand this statement. The king was with them—in their midst.

Another factor that people point to is the parables that point to a land-owner going away on a journey.

But He began to tell the people this parable: "A man planted a vineyard and leased it to vine-growers, and went on a journey for a long time. At the harvest time he sent a slave to the vine-growers, so that they would give him his share of the produce of the vineyard; but the vine-growers beat him and sent him away empty-handed. And he proceeded to send another slave; but they beat him also and treated him shamefully, and sent him away empty-handed. And he proceeded to send a third; but this one too they wounded and threw out. Now the owner of the vineyard said, 'What am I to do? I will send my beloved son; perhaps they will respect him.' But when the vine-growers saw him, they discussed with one another, saying, 'This is the heir; let's kill him so that the inheritance will be ours.' And so they threw him out of the vineyard and killed him. What, then, will the owner of the vineyard do to them? He will come and put these vine-growers to death, and will give the vineyard to others." However, when they heard this, they said, "May it never happen!" (Luke 20:9–16)

Some people understand these parables to be teaching that God is rejecting the Jews as His people and turning all the promised blessings over to the Gentiles who became Christians instead. An obvious rebuttal to this view is that God promised repeatedly throughout His Word, and Scripture cannot be broken, that He would *never abandon Israel as His chosen people.* Here's just one example.

This is what the Lord says, He who gives the sun for light by day and the fixed order of the moon and the stars for light by night, who stirs up the sea so that its waves roar—the Lord of armies is His name: "If this fixed order departs from Me," declares the Lord, "then the descendants of Israel also will cease to be a nation before Me forever." This is what the Lord says: "If the heavens above can be measured and the foundations of the earth searched out below, then I will also reject all the descendants of Israel for everything that they have done," declares the Lord. (Jeremiah 31:35–37)

God will not reject Israel as His people or replace them with another group. Instead, God expanded the concept of Israel by allowing Gentiles to partner with Israel as the greater people of God. Consider this: if God broke His promises to Israel, He would no longer be the protective and faithful God the Bible says He is.

What do these parables mean then? Who is God rejecting and replacing? A clue can be found in Luke 20:19, which says this: "And the chief priests and the scribes the same hour sought to lay hands on him; and they feared the people: for they perceived that he had spoken this parable against them" (KJV). The teachers knew Jesus had spoken this parable against them. He was saying that this group of leaders who would condemn him to death would be replaced by another group of leaders of Israel in the future who would repent and recognize Jesus as God's chosen Messiah as foretold by Zechariah.

And I will pour out on the house of David and on the inhabitants of Jerusalem the Spirit of grace and of pleading, so that they will look at Me whom they pierced; and they will mourn for Him, like one mourning for an only son, and they will weep bitterly over Him like the bitter weeping over a firstborn. On that day the mourning in Jerusalem will be great, like the mourning of Hadadrimmon in the plain of Megiddo. (Zech. 12:10–11)

Later, Paul, one of Jesus' followers, describes this in his letter to the Romans:

And so all Israel shall be saved: as it is written, There shall come out of Sion the Deliverer, and shall turn away ungodliness from Jacob: for this is my covenant unto them, when I shall take away their sins. (Rom. 11:26 –27 KJV)

All of these objections are consistent with the position that early

Christianity took at the end of the first century in response to the *Fiscus Judaicus* when they distanced themselves from Judaism and abandoned adherence to God's Law. However, these objections are contrary to the Judaism that Jesus taught, and which was taught by all of his immediate followers. Jesus' message never wavered from the message of the Hebrew Scriptures, unchanged and still relevant to our understanding today.

QUESTIONS

1.   What are some problems with interpreting Mark 7 as saying that "Jesus declared all foods clean"?

2.   What was Jesus' response when people accused him of breaking the Sabbath by healing people?

3.   How do we know God did not reject the Jews as His people?

4.   Who did Jesus indicate would be replaced in his parable of the vineyard?

CHAPTER 9

The Passion

At some point in Jesus' ministry—after urging people to repent and teaching that the establishment of God's ultimate kingdom was at hand as well as identifying himself as its king, Jesus realized that, although many were following him and believing his claims, virtually all the Jewish leaders opposed him. His offer of the kingdom would not be accepted voluntarily, and he would not oppose the Romans as well as the priesthood and make himself king by force.

There seems to be a shift in his message at this juncture. He pulled back on messages about the promised kingdom, at least as an imminent event, and started telling his disciples that he was going to be killed, and then rise from the dead. This was an abrupt change, and the disciples were startled, not knowing whether or not they should believe it. Were they understanding him correctly?

The key transition point, at least according to the synoptic Gospels, was when Jesus asked his disciples who they thought he was. Peter spoke up immediately, saying, "You are the Christ!" (Matt. 16:16). Peter directly said Jesus was the Messiah, the son of David, the long–awaited ruler who would regather Israel. Jesus affirmed that answer in the strongest possible terms. Peter's words are the kernel of the apostles' message throughout the Book of Acts.

Jesus still considered himself king of the kingdom yet to come. That never changed. Ironically, on the heels of that confession, Jesus began teaching his disciples that he would be killed and rise again after three days; the kingdom would now be delayed. We will discuss the implications of this delay in the next chapter. But for now, Jesus was apparently switching to plan B, which God had put in place from the beginning.

....

Suddenly, Jesus went from promised king to a criminal's death.

....

And what a dramatic switch this was! Suddenly, Jesus went from promised king to a criminal's death. Peter, as the spokesman for the disciples, protested. This was not what they had signed up for. Peter's reaction was understandable, but Jesus rebuked him and told him that he didn't have the things of God in mind. Apparently, Jesus' death was part of the necessary plan of God.

But why? Why was it necessary for Jesus to die and rise again? Jesus never gave an interpretation of his passion during the post–resurrection days, as least none that was recorded in the Gospels. We're dependent on the information contained in the letters written by his followers for that. They share that the death of Jesus was a substitutionary sacrifice for sinners. Everyone whom God, in His mercy, chooses to forgive, is forgiven based on the merit of the death of Jesus. This allowed God to be both just and merciful, because the penalty for sin was already paid by Jesus.

It's not clear at what point Jesus first knew about this change in plan. It's clear that he was not omniscient, as he pointed out that he did not know the time of his return.[1] However, he may have known about this plan earlier in his ministry and chosen not to focus on it. We don't really know.

It's clear that God knew about it from eternity, as there are allusions to it from the first chapters of Genesis. Speaking to the serpent, representing the evil one, God said, "And I will make enemies of you and the woman, and of your offspring and her Descendant; He shall bruise you on the head, and you shall bruise Him on the heel" (Gen. 3:15). At some point in the future, God told the Devil that the seed of a woman, a human being, would crush his head, although that person would be bitten in the heel by the evil one in the process.

There are a few mentions in the Gospel of John that could be understood as Jesus knowing about this plan at the beginning of his ministry, but there is certainly nothing in the synoptic Gospels to that effect. Also, chronology in John is at times very different than in the others. For example, in John 2, Jesus clears the temple of the money–changers, an event which doesn't occur until the end of Jesus' ministry in Matthew 21. Immediately afterward in John, Jesus says, "Destroy this temple, and in three days I will raise it up. (John 2:19 KJV). This statement dovetails with Jesus' discourse in Matthew 24 about the temple being destroyed. The point is that John may not have been relating things in the same chronological sequence as Matthew, Mark, and Luke. He did write at a much later date than the other three.

Immediately after Jesus started telling his disciples about his upcoming death, there is an event called the Mount of Transfiguration. Jesus took three of his disciples and led them up a high mountain to pray. While they were there, Jesus' face and clothes became bright with light, and

---

1 See Mark 13:32.

Moses and Elijah both appeared and spoke with him. The specific choice of Moses and Elijah seems to be an affirmation of the Law and the Prophets, represented by Moses and Elijah. Luke 9:31 says that they were talking about Jesus' departure, which he was about to fulfill in Jerusalem. If this is referring to his death, maybe they were bringing some additional information from God too. However, they could also have been referring to his ascension, which occurred a few weeks later.

It's true that in Matthew's account, Jesus gave a hint of his death when he spoke of the sign of the prophet Jonah: "For just as Jonah was in the stomach of a sea monster for three days and three nights, so will the Son of Man be in the heart of the earth for three days and three nights" (Matt. 12:40). A few chapters later in Matthew 16:4, Jesus told people seeking a sign that only "the sign of Jonah" would be given to them. This occurred *before* Matthew's account in chapter 16 of Peter's confession and Jesus' change of message. However, in Luke the account of Peter's confession occurs in chapter 9, *prior* to the account of the sign of Jonah in Luke 11:30, so it all depends on which one has the story in the correct chronological order.

In any event, all four Gospels view the death and resurrection of Jesus as the climax and culmination of his story. As it happened, Jesus and his disciples were going to Jerusalem for the festival of Passover in obedience to the command in Deuteronomy 16:16 as previously mentioned.

Several days before Passover, Jesus entered Jerusalem riding on the colt of a donkey, which was another sign of the promised Messiah. The prophet Zechariah wrote: "Rejoice greatly, O daughter of Zion; shout, O daughter of Jerusalem: behold, thy King cometh unto thee: he is just, and having salvation; lowly, and riding upon an ass, and upon a colt the foal of an ass" (Zech. 9:9 KJV). Many people in Jerusalem (as well as those coming for the feast) recognized this sign and gathered to cheer him, shouting,

"Hosanna to the son of David: Blessed is he that cometh in the name of the Lord; hosanna in the highest" (Matt. 21:9 KJV) which is also found in Psalm 118:25–26.

While crowds of people believed Jesus' claim and cheered him as Messiah, the priests and religious leaders opposed him and his message, and increasingly viewed Jesus as a problem they needed to contain as the days wore on. They wanted to have him arrested, but so many people considered Jesus a true prophet, or quite possibly even the Messiah, that the Jewish leaders were afraid. Therefore they planned to arrest him secretly at night when it would be less noticeable. They plotted with one of Jesus' disciples, Judas, to identify him for them just before Passover.

On the eve of Passover, Jesus met with his disciples in an upper room to commemorate the festival. It's uncertain how many of the traditions of the Passover Seder were in place at that time, but it certainly involved unleavened bread and cups of wine. Jesus did much teaching at the Seder, as he had in the previous days. One of the things he did with his disciples at this Passover meal was to expand the symbolism involved in it. Knowing that he was to die in the immediate future, he pointed out that the unleavened bread, in addition to symbolizing the quick exodus from Egypt, would also be a symbol of his body that was to be broken (and hidden away). The cup of wine after supper would symbolize his blood, which was to be shed for all mankind through his death. He told his disciples that whenever they celebrated Passover, they should remember his death when they ate the unleavened bread and drank the cup of wine.

After the evening meal, and much teaching, Jesus and his disciples walked to the garden of Gethsemane at the foot of the Mount of Olives, where Jesus prayed and the disciples fell asleep. Jesus prayed that if possible he could escape what he knew was coming. However, he also knew that God had ordained it as part of His plan.

As they were leaving Gethsemane, a group of priests, elders, and officers of the temple guard came to arrest him. Judas came up and kissed him, identifying Jesus as the one they came to arrest. The guards brought Jesus to the Sanhedrin, the "supreme judicial and ecclesiastical council of ancient Jerusalem"[2] where he was asked whether he was the Messiah. He answered, "It is as you said" (Matt. 26:64, NKJV). They were all shocked and accused him of blasphemy. Then they sent him to Pilate, the Roman governor, since the Jewish leaders didn't have Roman permission to pronounce a death sentence.

Pilate also asked Jesus if he was the king of the Jews. Once again, Jesus affirmed that he was.[3] At that point, the Jewish leaders present began accusing Jesus of various charges, but he didn't answer. Pilate wanted to release Jesus, but the crowd that was gathered demanded his blood. Incidentally, this was not the same crowd that had welcomed Jesus as he entered the city a short time before. These were mostly priests and temple officials, not representatives of the Jewish people.

Pilate was in the habit of releasing one prisoner at the time of the feast. He asked the crowd whether he should release Jesus or a notorious criminal named Barabbas. The crowd cried for Barabbas. When Pilate asked what he should do with Jesus, they shouted, "Crucify him!" Pilate could have stood against them and released Jesus, but like so many leaders, he gave in to the pressure of the crowd.

The Roman soldiers beat and stripped Jesus, put a crown of thorns on his head, and led him out to be crucified. They nailed him to a cross and left him there to die. Pilate insisted that they post a sign: "Pilate also wrote an inscription and put it on the cross. It was written: JESUS THE

---

2 WordNet 3.0, Farlex clipart collection. S.v. "Sanhedrin." Retrieved June 5, 2023, from https://www.thefreedictionary.com/Sanhedrin

3 See Matthew 27:11.

NAZARENE, THE KING OF THE JEWS'" (John 19:19). Perhaps this was a last ditch effort to relieve himself of his responsibility for his decision.

After several hours of hanging on the cross, Jesus died. The gospel accounts differ about what he said on the cross, but he appears to have asked God for forgiveness for the people that were killing him.[4] The priests were in a hurry to get the men off the crosses because the next day was a Sabbath, which in their reckoning started at sunset the evening before, so a soldier went to the three people being crucified to make sure they were dead, and break their legs if they were not. However, Jesus was already dead, so they didn't break his legs.

The Sabbath on the following day was either the weekly Sabbath (seventh day) or the festival Sabbath; it's not entirely clear. The festival of Unleavened Bread may have started on Thursday or Friday, but in any event, Jesus was taken down from the cross. A rich follower of Jesus named Joseph asked for his body, wrapped it, and placed it in a tomb that he owned, and had never been used. Joseph had a stone rolled in front of the door, and the Romans set a guard at the tomb, so no one would steal the body.

Some of the women who had followed Jesus wanted to anoint the body with spices, but they had listened to Jesus' teaching for a long time and knew that they should not do work on the Sabbath. They rested in obedience to the commandment.[5] As soon as the Sabbath was over—sunset on Saturday—they set out with their spices to anoint Jesus' body. The account in Matthew 28:1, if translated according to the normal meanings of the Greek words, would be rendered thus: "Late on the Sabbath, as the first day of the week was approaching," meaning Saturday evening. Matthew

4 See Luke 23:34.
5 See Luke 23:56.

is the only one of the Gospels that recounts the actual moment of the resurrection, with the earthquake and the angel rolling back the stone. The other Gospels relate the results of the resurrection, things that happened later, which seem to take place on Sunday morning. However, according to Matthew's account, the actual resurrection occurred shortly after sunset on Saturday evening.

Christians in subsequent centuries decided to turn Sunday into a holy day and ignore the Sabbath God commanded the Jews. They did this because Jesus was supposedly raised on Sunday. However, Jesus spoke of being three days and three nights in the heart of the earth as the sign of Jonah. He was removed from the cross on a late afternoon. The only way it could be timed to make it three days and three nights is for the resurrection to be on Saturday evening and the burial to have been on Wednesday evening, with Thursday as the Festival Sabbath. Of course, Jesus was raised on the day after the Sabbath; he was resting on the Sabbath. Jesus would never have approved of people making his resurrection day into a holy day, a replacement for the Sabbath. Instead, it was an affirmation that Jesus kept the Mosaic Law and rested on the Sabbath.

After his resurrection, Jesus appeared to many of his disciples over a period of forty days, after which he was taken up in a cloud to heaven. As far as we know, he didn't give his followers any interpretation of the meaning of his death and resurrection. And that is where we'll pick up next.

QUESTIONS

1.   How did Jesus' message change toward the end of his life?

2.   How can God be both just and merciful toward sinners?

3.   Which of the four Gospels seems to be relating events in a different chronological sequence than the others?

4.   Who appeared to Jesus and his disciples on the Mount of Transfiguration?

5.   During his trial, what did Jesus affirm?

6. Why did the women not anoint Jesus' body immediately after his death?

7. Who claimed Jesus' body and placed it in a new tomb?

8. How did Jesus keep the ultimate Sabbath rest?

CHAPTER 10

Restore the Kingdom?

Shortly after Jesus' resurrection, his disciples "gathered around him and asked him, 'Lord, are you at this time going to restore the kingdom to Israel?' He said to them: 'It is not for you to know the times or dates the Father has set by his own authority'" (Acts 1:6–7). Basically, Jesus said, "Not now." He had been teaching them (and all his listeners) for his entire ministry that the promised kingdom was at hand and he was its king. Now he tells them that he's going away, and the kingdom won't be established for a while yet. His followers thought it would be soon. We know now that it was going to be thousands of years. The kingdom the prophets predicted was going to be delayed. After Jesus ascended, angels came and told the disciples that Jesus would return the same way they saw him leave.

Did this make him a failed Messiah? In a sense, you could think of it like that. However, the failure was on the part of the leaders who rejected Jesus' teaching and claims, not Jesus. It's true that the role of Messiah, the anointed king of restored Israel, was not one Jesus accomplished during his life. In that sense, he was not the Messiah, but he was the person who would *be the Messiah in time.* That's what the faith of his disciples focused on and what they taught to the people in Acts. And it required faith.

We need to realize that just as the lifestyle and message of Jesus were *very* Jewish and in accordance with the Hebrew Scriptures, so also was the idea of his message as Messiah being rejected. That and the fact that he would return at a later time as Messiah is modeled many times in the Hebrew Scriptures. It's a very Jewish idea when you stop to think about it.

Perhaps the most obvious model is the one we looked at previously: the life of Joseph, son of Jacob in Genesis. Joseph's dreams of the family bowing down to him parallels with Jesus announcing himself as Messiah. Just like Jesus, Joseph's message was totally rejected and he was metaphorically killed by his own brothers, though he was actually sold to slave traders. Joseph's father was told that Joseph was dead. Yet, many years later Joseph became a ruler in Egypt and the savior of his own people. His brothers didn't recognize him at first when they saw him, but when Joseph told them who he was, it all made sense. They did bow to him. In fact, they had done that before they even knew it was Joseph! Later, they even moved to the land Joseph oversaw.

However, when he reveals himself, they will embrace him.

When Jesus returns, his Israelite brothers may not recognize him at first either. However, when he reveals himself, they will embrace him. They are expecting a Messiah; they just don't know who he will be. If it turns out to be a brother they have mistreated in the past, they will be ashamed of their actions, but that won't stop them from welcoming him as their king.

In Jewish tradition, there are a number of references to a Messiah son of Joseph in addition to the messiah son of David. This son of Joseph is to come first and die, then be resurrected as the son of David comes to reign. In the typical Jewish understanding, these are two different people. But maybe not. It might be of significance that the name of Jesus' stepfather was Joseph. It seems to be through Joseph that Jesus' lineage is traced back to David, as Mary seems to be related to the tribe of Levi. Though Jesus was not physically the son of Joseph, maybe he was the son of Joseph in the sense of fulfilling the imagery portrayed by the life of Joseph in Genesis. I highly recommend the book, *Messiah ben Joseph*, by David C. Mitchell, which discusses every mention in Jewish literature of this Messiah ben Joseph. It's a fascinating study.

There are also other models of Jesus' delayed kingship in the Old Testament. They are typically more partial of a model than Joseph's, but they are all previews we can recognize as hints of what is to come. One of these is Noah. During the years Noah was building the ark, he pleaded with people to repent. Genesis does not tell us about this, but in 2 Peter 2:5, Noah is called a "preacher of righteousness." Noah's preaching was rejected even more than Jesus' was. God was willing to save no one beyond Noah's family from the flood. The ark, which was their place of refuge from the coming judgment could be considered as a metaphor of Jesus and the salvation provided by his death.

Another fairly limited model of Jesus is Abraham. His father, Terah, set out from Ur to go to Canaan, taking Abram, his wife Sarai, and his nephew Lot. However, they stopped when they were partway there in Haran. Apparently, they stayed in Haran for some time. While they were there, Terah died. At some later date, God again called Abram to leave his home and go to Canaan, the land God would promise to His progeny for all time. The two journeys could be considered a model for Jesus' two visits to earth: one in the past in which someone dies at the end, and one in the future in which Israel is regathered to their land.

Another model, not so much of the delay but of the passion of Jesus, is Abraham's son, Isaac, in the event referred to as the *Akedah*, the binding of Isaac. God told Abraham to take Isaac and sacrifice him on a mountain. God had already told Abraham that Isaac would be the source of countless progeny, so it's natural that Abraham would be confused by this command, just as the disciples of Jesus were confused after understanding that Jesus was the coming Davidic king, and then being told that their king had to die. Abraham trusted God and obeyed Him. He had Isaac carry the wood for the sacrifice just as Jesus carried the cross.[1] Interestingly, it was a three-day walk to the place of sacrifice. As Abraham raised his knife to kill Isaac, at the last moment, an angel called for him to stop. This was metaphorically a death and a resurrection, just as Joseph's release from the pit was. A ram was provided to be sacrificed instead of Isaac. This models the substitutionary atonement that Jesus provided, dying in place of sinners so God could justly forgive them.

Another clear model of Jesus is the situation with Moses. Moses was raised in Pharaoh's household and showed great promise of becoming a ruler himself. However, Moses stood up for a Hebrew and killed an Egyptian and hid the act, so Pharaoh tried to have him killed instead. He didn't succeed, but the attempt parallels the death of Jesus. Moses fled and lived a long time in a distant land, but eventually God sent him back to redeem Israel and lead them out of Egypt. In a similar way, God will send Messiah to establish Israel in its own land. Another possible model for Messiah's delay is also found in the life of Moses. Moses was not permitted to enter the Promised Land after forty years in the wilderness.

---

1 See John 19:17.

Instead, Moses died on a mountain overlooking the land. Centuries later, Moses appeared with Jesus and Elijah on the Mount of Transfiguration. In that way, Moses made it into the Promised Land after all. God had promised that He would send a prophet like Moses to Israel to tell them what to do. That is one of the roles Jesus played while on earth.

Another model is Hoshea, the servant of Moses, who was renamed Joshua, which is, interestingly, the Hebrew equivalent of the name that we know as Jesus. Joshua entered the land of Canaan as a spy. Then he had to wander in the desert for forty years before becoming leader of Israel at the death of Moses. He led the nation into the land God had promised them, and ruled over them for many years, overseeing the division of the land among the tribes.

Another clear model of the Messiah is King David. Throughout the prophets David is used as a stand–in for the Messiah. An example of this is in Jeremiah:

"It shall come about on that day,'" declares the Lord of armies, "that I will break his yoke from their necks and will tear to pieces their restraints; and strangers will no longer make them their slaves. But they shall serve the Lord their God and David their king, whom I will raise up for them." (Jeremiah 30:8–9)

It's clear from many passages that it would not be David himself, but one of his descendants who would reign over this ultimate kingdom. The delay is illustrated by the fact that David was anointed for the kingship by Samuel when he was just a young boy, years before he was actually made king. During those intervening years, Saul tried to kill him, and almost succeeded, perhaps paralleling the death of Jesus. However, many years later, after proving himself an outstanding warrior, David became king of all of Israel, serving as an example of a future time when all Israel will be regathered and united. It was to David that God made the promise that "thine house and thy kingdom shall be established for ever before thee: thy throne shall be established for ever" (2 Sam. 7:16 KJV). This promise was echoed by the prophets.

Another example of the delayed Messiah is Elijah. He was called as a prophet and for many years, Elijah preached repentance and stood up for righteousness. He did miracles, including multiplying food, and even raised a widow's son from the dead, as did Jesus. Lastly, Elijah was taken up to heaven in a whirlwind without dying. And, of course, centuries later, he appeared with Jesus and Moses on the Mount of Transfiguration. Elijah is connected especially to the coming of the Messiah because it was predicted that a prophet like him would return to earth before the coming of Messiah to prepare God's people.

Behold, I am going to send you Elijah the prophet before the coming of the great and terrible day of the LORD. He will turn the hearts of the fathers back to their children and the hearts of the children to their fathers, so that I will not come and strike the land with complete destruction. (Malachi 4:5–6)

John the Baptist represented Elijah for the coming of Jesus, but John denied that he was Elijah.[2] Nevertheless, Jesus said that he *was* the Elijah–yet–to–come—a miracle worker of the past. The original Elijah had been taken to heaven by God, and was expected to return in connection with the establishment of the kingdom of God. This clearly paralleled with the life of Jesus.

---

2 See John 1:21.

And His disciples asked Him, "Why then do the scribes say that Elijah must come first?" And He answered and said, "Elijah is coming and will restore all things; but I say to you that Elijah already came, and they did not recognize him, but did to him whatever they wanted. So also the Son of Man is going to suffer at their hands." Then the disciples understood that He had spoken to them about John the Baptist. (Matt. 17:10–13)

The stone tablets Moses received on Mt. Sinai with the Ten Commandments inscribed by God's finger also contain an interesting parallel with the delayed Messiah, one not based on a person. When Moses went down and saw the people worshiping a golden calf, he threw the tablets down and broke them, perhaps modeling the death of Jesus, who had God's message. Moses went up the mountain again and received God's imprint on a second set of stone tablets. These were permanent, and were kept in the ark of the covenant that always traveled with Israel, and was first housed in the holy of holies in the tabernacle and later in the temple.

The last thing to discuss in this chapter is not really a model of the delayed Messiah, but an extended passage in Isaiah that seems to predict the sufferings of Jesus and their significance as a substitute for sinners. Isaiah presents a figure that he calls "the servant of the Lord." At times, this servant is identified as Israel, but other times Isaiah seems to portray an individual that represents the nation.

The Jews have tended to downplay these passages and insist that they only refer to Israel as a nation. This is understandable, as Jews have been persecuted and killed by Christians throughout history. However, it's a very Jewish mode of interpretation to take something that is portrayed literally and have it also act as a metaphor for something else. Having the servant act as both the nation of Israel and an individual representing that nation is a very Jewish thing to do.

We've already seen this in the birth narratives in which Jesus is portrayed as representing Israel. Matthew paralleled Jesus leaving Egypt as a young child with the exodus under Moses when he quoted Hosea 11:1 when he wrote, "Out of Egypt I called my son" in Matthew 2:15. It's interesting to note that the first time "the servant" in Isaiah is introduced, he is identified as Israel:

> But you, Israel, My servant, Jacob whom I have chosen, Descendant of Abraham My friend, you whom I have taken from the ends of the earth and called from its remotest parts, and said to you, "You are My servant, I have chosen you and have not rejected you. Do not fear, for I am with you; do not be afraid, for I am your God. I will strengthen you, I will also help you, I will also uphold you with My righteous right hand." (Isa. 41:8–10)

Soon after this though, the servant is described in a way that sounds like it is referring to an individual.

> Behold, My Servant, whom I uphold; My chosen one in whom My soul delights. I have put My Spirit upon Him; He will bring forth justice to the nations. He will not cry out nor raise His voice, nor make His voice heard in the street. A bent reed He will not break off and a dimly burning wick He will not extinguish; He will faithfully bring forth justice. (Isa. 42:1–3)

This could still be referring to national Israel, but it makes us wonder about other options because of the intense personification in the passage. The next five passages seem to surely refer to Israel, with the second one taking Israel to task for not following the Law.

Hear, you who are deaf! And look, you who are blind, so that you may see. Who is blind but My servant, or so deaf as My messenger whom I send? Who is so blind as one who is at peace with Me, or so blind as the servant of the Lord? You have seen many things, but you do not retain them; your ears are open, but no one hears. (Isa. 42:18–20)

The Lord was pleased for His righteousness' sake to make the Law great and glorious.... Who gave Jacob up for spoils, and Israel to plunderers? Was it not the Lord, against whom we have sinned, and in whose ways they were not willing to walk, and whose Law they did not obey? (Isa. 42:21, 24)

But now listen, Jacob, My servant, and Israel, whom I have chosen: This is what the Lord says, He who made you and formed you from the womb, who will help you: "Do not fear, Jacob My servant, and Jeshurun, whom I have chosen. For I will pour water on the thirsty land and streams on the dry ground; I will pour out My Spirit on your offspring, and My blessing on your descendants; and they will spring up among the grass like poplars by streams of water." This one will say, "I am the Lord's"; and that one will call on the name of Jacob; and another will write on his hand, "Belonging to the Lord," and will give himself Israel's name with honor. (Isa. 44:1–5)

"Remember these things, Jacob, and Israel, for you are My servant; I have formed you, you are My servant, Israel, you will not be forgotten by Me. I have wiped out your wrongdoings like a thick cloud and your sins like a heavy mist. Return to Me, for I have redeemed you." Shout for joy, you heavens, for the Lord has done it! Shout joyfully, you lower parts of the earth; break into a shout of jubilation, you mountains, forest, and every tree in it; for the Lord has redeemed Jacob, and in Israel He shows His glory. (Isa. 44:21–23)

For the sake of Jacob My servant, and Israel My chosen one, I have also called you by your name; I have given you a title of honor though you have not known Me. (Isa. 45:4)

The servant mentioned in chapter 49 seems to be Israel at first, but then immediately and obviously transitions to an individual.

And now says the Lord, who formed Me from the womb to be His Servant, to bring Jacob back to Him, so that Israel might be gathered to Him (for I am honored in the sight of the Lord, and My God is My strength), He says, "It is too small a thing that You should be My Servant to raise up the tribes of Jacob and to restore the protected ones of Israel; I will also make You a light of the nations so that My salvation may reach to the end of the earth." (Isa. 49:5–6)

In this instance, the servant is restoring the tribes of Israel, as well as being a light to the Gentiles. The main section that seems to refer to the servant as an individual and also parallels the sufferings of Jesus is Isaiah 52:13–53:12.

Behold, My Servant will prosper, He will be high and lifted up and greatly exalted. Just as many were appalled at you, My people, so His appearance was marred beyond that of a man, and His form beyond the sons of mankind. So He will sprinkle many nations, kings will shut their mouths on account of Him; for what they had not been told, they will see, and what they had not heard, they will understand.

Who has believed our report? And to whom has the arm of the Lord been revealed? For He grew up before Him like a tender shoot, and like a root out of dry ground; He has no stately form or majesty that we would look at Him, nor an appearance that we would take pleasure in Him. He was despised and abandoned by men, a man of great pain and familiar with sickness; and like one from whom people hide their faces, He was despised, and we had no regard for Him.

However, it was our sicknesses that He Himself bore, and our pains that He carried; yet we ourselves assumed that He had been afflicted, struck down by God, and humiliated, but He was pierced for our offenses, He was crushed for our wrongdoings; the punishment for our well–being was laid upon Him, and by His wounds we are healed. All of us, like sheep, have gone astray, each of us has turned to his own way; but the Lord has caused the wrongdoing of us all to fall on Him.

He was oppressed and afflicted, yet He did not open His mouth; like a lamb that is led to slaughter, and like a sheep that is silent before its shearers, so He did not open His mouth. By oppression and judgment He was taken away; and as for His generation, who considered that He was cut off from the land of the living for the wrongdoing of my people, to whom the blow was due? And His grave was assigned with wicked men, yet He was with a rich man in His death, because He had done no violence, nor was there any deceit in His mouth. But the Lord desired to crush Him, causing Him grief; if He renders Himself as a guilt offering, He will see His offspring, He will prolong His days, and the good pleasure of the Lord will prosper in His hand. As a result of the anguish of His soul, He will see it and be satisfied; by His knowledge the Righteous One, My Servant, will justify the many, for He will bear their wrongdoings. Therefore, I will allot Him a portion with the great, and He will divide the plunder with the strong, because He poured out His life unto death, and was counted with wrongdoers; yet He Himself bore the sin of many, and interceded for the wrongdoers. (Isa. 52:13–53:12)

Several details are pointed out regarding the suffering servant in this passage: he was despised. He was killed for our sins. He was buried, but raised to receive a portion among the great. All this was according to God's will. In fact, this passage encapsulates Christ's complete mission and the gospel message.

Isaiah 53 is not alone in foretelling these events down to many small details. In a similar way, Psalm 22 corresponds to the crucifixion of Jesus too. Jesus recited a phrase from Psalm 22 when he was on the cross, but the whole psalm is a description of his experience.

These details are so exact a description of Jesus' experience that taken with all the other prophecies regarding Messiah that Jesus fulfilled, it's hard not to believe Jesus is the predicted Messiah he claimed to be. Others claimed that he was too—even after he died! They attested to the fact that once the Jewish leaders had rejected Jesus' claim to Messiah, he had died to substitute himself for the sin of all people, after which, he was resurrected and ascended to heaven. His followers preached that Jesus would return at some point to finally establish the promised kingdom. All these things are modeled many times in the Hebrew Scriptures, and each of these details are perfectly in accord with biblical Judaism.

QUESTIONS

1. What did the disciples ask Jesus about the kingdom shortly after his resurrection?

2. How did he answer them?

3. What did the angel tell the disciples after Jesus ascended?

4. How does the story of Joseph in Genesis symbolize the departure and return of Jesus?

5. What other events or people in the Hebrew Scriptures can represent the rejection, death, and return of Jesus?

6.   How do the stone tablets that Moses received picture the death and return of Messiah?

7.   In what ways does the "servant of the Lord" in Isaiah parallel the experiences of Jesus?

8.   How can this "servant" represent both Israel as a nation and the suffering Messiah?

CHAPTER 11

The Message of the Apostles

It's a pretty easy job to portray the disciples of Jesus as adherents of Judaism after the ascension, as the trend among Bible scholars has been to understand them as such. They clearly centered their worship and ministry around the temple in Jerusalem. In the description of the lifestyle of the early believers at the end of Acts 2, we are told, "and they, continuing daily with one accord in the temple" (Acts 2:46 KJV). Their time in the temple was presumably at the times of prayer—the third and the ninth hour.

An example of this occurs only a few verses later. "Now Peter and John went up together into the temple at the hour of prayer, being the ninth hour" (Acts 3:1 KJV). On this particular daily visit to the temple, Peter and John encountered a lame man begging at the temple gate. They healed him; and when a crowd gathered, they preached about Jesus, saying he was the promised Messiah that would be coming back to reign. Their plea to the listeners was: "Repent, then, and turn to God," (an echo of what Jesus taught), "turning away every one of you from his iniquities" (Acts 3:26 KJV). Even after extensive persecution by the temple authorities, they continued teaching in the temple: "And daily in the temple, and in every house, they ceased not to teach and preach Jesus Christ" (Acts 5:42 KJV).

One of the early believers, Stephen, drew opposition from some Jews because of the power with which he spoke about Jesus.

But some men from what was called the Synagogue of the Freedmen, including both Cyrenians and Alexandrians, and some from Cilicia and Asia, rose up and argued with Stephen. But they were unable to cope with his wisdom and the Spirit by whom he was speaking. Then they secretly induced men to say, "We have heard him speak blasphemous words against Moses and God." And they stirred up the people, the elders, and the scribes, and they came up to him and dragged him away, and brought him before the Council. They put forward false witnesses who said, "This man does not stop speaking against this holy place and the Law; for we have heard him say that this Nazarene, Jesus, will destroy this place and change the customs which Moses handed down to us." (Acts 6:9–14)

These opponents are clearly identified as false witnesses when they make claims that Stephen was speaking against the temple and the Law. In fact, after a lengthy speech, in which he recounts the history of Israel, Stephen accuses them of not obeying the Law.

You men who are stiff-necked and uncircumcised in heart and ears are always resisting the Holy Spirit; you are doing just as your fathers did. Which one of the prophets did your fathers not persecute? They killed those who had previously announced the coming of the Righteous One, and you have now become betrayers and murderers of Him; you who received the Law as ordained by angels, and yet did not keep it. (Acts 7:51–53)

This was similar to Jesus' accusation in John 7:19, when he said, "Did Moses not give you the Law, and yet none of you carries out the Law?" However, the people were angry enough with Stephen that they picked up rocks and stoned him to death, a death the future Paul witnessed and condoned.

Another occasion that illustrates the religious bent of the apostles occurs in Acts 10 when Peter had a vision.

On the next day, as they were on their way and approaching the city, Peter went up on the housetop about the sixth hour to pray. But he became hungry and wanted to eat; but while they were making preparations, he fell into a trance; and he saw the sky opened up, and an object like a great sheet coming down, lowered by four corners to the ground, and on it were all kinds of four-footed animals and crawling creatures of the earth and birds of the sky. A voice came to him, "Get up, Peter, kill and eat!" But Peter said, "By no means, Lord, for I have never eaten anything unholy and unclean." Again a voice came to him a second time, "What God has cleansed, no longer consider unholy." This happened three times, and immediately the object was taken up into the sky. Now while Peter was greatly perplexed in mind as to what the vision which he had seen might mean, behold, the men who had been sent by Cornelius had asked directions to Simon's house, and they appeared at the gate. (Acts 10:9–17)

There are many key facts in this story that help us understand it. First of all, Peter refused to disobey the commands he followed carefully regarding eating, even when he heard a strange voice telling him to do so.[1] In referring to the voice as "Lord," he was not acknowledging it as God. The Greek word translated "Lord" can simply be a respectful form

---

1 See Leviticus 11 and Deuteronomy 14.

of address, like the Spanish señor. He refused three times to do what the voice asked, knowing that he was being faithful to God's commands. Peter was not thinking that the Old Testament commands were obsolete, as later Christians conjectured.

....

Peter didn't immediately jump to the conclusion that this vision was about canceling the food laws.

....

The passage states that Peter "doubted in himself what this vision which he had seen should mean" (Acts 10:17 KJV). Peter didn't immediately jump to the conclusion that this vision was about canceling the food laws. Later he realized the meaning of the vision wasn't about food at all, but people. "God has shown me that I am not to call any person unholy or unclean" (Acts 10:28). As a result, he visited a Gentile centurion, who feared the God of Israel, and told him about Jesus. It's interesting that Peter, who had been with Jesus for his entire ministry, still felt so strongly about obeying God's laws. Clearly Jesus had not taught his disciples anything contrary.

Acts 15 is sometimes misunderstood. As more and more Gentiles were embracing Jesus as Messiah, the question arose of whether they should convert to Judaism and follow the Mosaic Law. Three actions were required for conversion to Judaism: circumcision (for men), immersion in water, and a pledge to obey Torah. "Circumcision" was used as a kind of shorthand term to refer to the entire process. Most of the time when we read about circumcision in the New Testament, it's referring to Gentiles converting to Judaism.

The apostles gathered and had a long discussion about this. They concluded that God brings Gentiles to faith as Gentiles, not Jews. The prophets had made many predictions about people from other nations embracing the God of Israel in the last days. If they all converted to Judaism, they would become Jews, and defeat the purpose of God in having followers among people from the nations. The apostles recognized that it would be a tremendous difficulty for a Gentile who was unfamiliar with God's commands to embrace the entire Law all at once. Instead, they introduced four laws: practices that would allow the Gentile Christians to be accepted in the Jewish community. Then as they learned more about the Scriptures, they could embrace more of God's commands at a pace they could accept. "For from ancient generations Moses has those who preach him in every city, since he is read in the synagogues every Sabbath" (Acts 15:21).

There is an event in Acts 21 that we will look at more fully when we discuss Paul, but suffice it to say, there was a community of thousands of believers in Jerusalem—all of whom were zealous for the Law. The apostles, and especially James, the brother of Jesus, who was the leader of the group, seemed proud of this fact. The believers had been told a false message about Paul, namely that he was teaching new believers not to follow Torah. Paul went to considerable effort to disprove this, and show that he was indeed living in obedience to the Law.

The letters we have in the New Testament by Jesus' early followers, Peter, James, and John, are very supportive of Torah and Judaism. James mentioned the law several times using complimentary terms. It is called "the perfect law of liberty" in James 1:25, the "the law of liberty" in 2:12, and "the royal law" in 2:8. Later James said this: "If thou judge the law, thou art not a doer of the law, but a judge" (James 4:11 KJV). Apparently, his readers *are supposed to be following the Law.* A primary emphasis in James is that we are not to merely listen to God's Word, but also obey it.

> *But prove yourselves doers of the word, and not just hearers who deceive themselves. For if anyone is a hearer of the word and not a doer, he is like a man who looks at his natural face in a mirror; for once he has looked at himself and gone away, he has immediately forgotten what kind of person he was. But one who has looked intently at the perfect law, the law of freedom, and has continued in it, not having become a forgetful hearer but an active doer, this person will be blessed in what he does. (James 1:22–25)*

James also wrote about faith without deeds.

> *What use is it, my brothers and sisters, if someone says he has faith, but he has no works? Can that faith save him? If a brother or sister is without clothing and in need of daily food, and one of you says to them, "Go in peace, be warmed and be filled," yet you do not give them what is necessary for their body, what use is that? In the same way, faith also, if it has no works, is dead, being by itself. But someone may well say, "You have faith and I have works; show me your faith without the works, and I will show you my faith by my works." You believe that God is one. You do well; the demons also believe, and shudder. But are you willing to acknowledge, you foolish person, that faith without works is useless? Was our father Abraham not justified by works when he offered up his son Isaac on the altar? You see that faith was working with his works, and as a result of the works, faith was perfected; and the Scripture was fulfilled which says, "and Abraham believed God, and it was credited to Him as righteousness," and he was called a friend of God. You see that a person is justified by works and not by faith alone. In the same way, was Rahab the*

The Message of the Apostles

prostitute not justified by works also when she received the messengers and sent them out by another way? For just as the body without the spirit is dead, so also faith without works is dead. (James 2:14–26)

The point of this passage is that if faith is real, it will be accompanied by good deeds. This is similar to what Jesus taught when he said, "You will know them by their fruits," which was the main point of his teaching on false prophets found in Matthew 7:15–23.

Another interesting point made by James is often obscured by translators. Translated literally, James 2:2, which is about treating the rich and poor alike, says, "Suppose a man comes into your synagogue...." Translators often render the word for synagogue as "meeting" or "assembly" to hide the fact that early believers met in synagogues, Jews and God–fearing Gentiles together. However, there is considerable evidence for that habit in the New Testament, some of which we'll see in the next chapter when we study Paul.

The letters of John are very friendly to Torah and Judaism as well. The main point John made in these letters is that love for God is revealed in obeying God's commands. Multiple passages bring this out. Here's an example:

By this we know that we have come to know Him, if we keep His commandments. The one who says, "I have come to know Him," and does not keep His commandments, is a liar, and the truth is not in him; but whoever follows His word, in him the love of God has truly been perfected. By this we know that we are in Him: the one who says that he remains in Him ought, himself also, walk just as He walked. (1 John 2:3–6)

In chapter 3, John defined sin as lawlessness.

Everyone who practices sin also practices lawlessness; and sin is lawlessness. You know that He appeared in order to take away sins; and in Him there is no sin. No one who remains in Him sins continually; no one who sins continually has seen Him or knows Him. Little children, make sure no one deceives you; the one who practices righteousness is righteous, just as He is righteous; the one who practices sin is of the devil; for the devil has been sinning from the beginning. The Son of God appeared for this purpose, to destroy the works of the devil. No one who has been born of God practices sin, because His seed remains in him; and he cannot sin continually, because he has been born of God. By this the children of God and the children of the devil are obvious: anyone who does not practice righteousness is not of God, nor the one who does not love his brother and sister. (1 John 3:4–10)

This is strong language, akin to what James said about deeds being the evidence of faith. Perhaps the strongest passage on this topic is found a little later:

By this we know that we love the children of God, when we love God and follow His commandments. For this is the love of God, that we keep His commandments; and His commandments are not burdensome. (1 John 5:2–3)

These verses allude to what Jesus said was a summary of the whole Law: loving God, the greatest commandment, and loving one's neighbor, which was similarly great. It's clear that loving God is exhibited by keeping the commands he gave to his people through Moses. This topic is mentioned briefly in 2 John as well.

I was overjoyed to find some of your children walking in truth, just as we have received a commandment to do from the Father. Now I ask you, lady, not as though I were writing to you a new commandment, but the one which we have had from the beginning, that we love one another. And this is love, that we walk according to His commandments. This is the commandment, just as you have heard from the beginning, that you are to walk in it. (2 John 4–6)

It is assumed that the same John that wrote the gospel of John and 1, 2, and 3 John also wrote Revelation. It's notable that twice in Revelation, the righteous are defined as "those which keep the commandments of God, and have the testimony of Jesus Christ" (Rev. 12, 14:17b KJV).[2] It's plain to see that both James and John endorsed the practice of keeping God's commands in Torah.

The epistles of Peter don't speak as specifically about God's commands in Torah, but 2 Peter does have some interesting things to say about Paul, which serves to introduce the next chapter.

Wherefore, beloved, seeing that ye look for such things, be diligent that ye may be found of him in peace, without spot, and blameless. And account that the longsuffering of our Lord is salvation; even as our beloved brother Paul also according to the wisdom given unto him hath written unto you; as also in all his epistles, speaking in them of these things; in which are some things hard to be understood, which they that are unlearned and unstable wrest, as they do also the other scriptures, unto their own destruction. Ye therefore, beloved, seeing ye know these things before, beware lest ye also, being led away with the error of the wicked [literally "lawless men"], fall from your own stedfastness. (2 Peter 3:14–17 KJV, addition mine)

Paul's letters *are* confusing and hard to understand, and those who misread them were in danger as these verses make clear. This "error of lawless men" has become overwhelming in the Christian church since the second century, presumably based on the teachings of Paul. We'll look into this more in the next chapter.

---

2 Also, see Revelation 14:12.

QUESTIONS

1. After Jesus ascended, where did his disciples conduct most of their worship?

2. What false claims did some people make against Stephen?

3. What accusation in Stephen's speech seemed to drive them to kill him?

4. Under what circumstance did Peter claim that he would not break the biblical dietary laws?

5. What laws were Gentile believers asked to follow in Acts 15?

6. What verse in Acts 15 suggests that Gentiles could embrace Torah gradually, as they learned about it?

7. In which city are we told in Acts 21 were there thousands of believers—all of whom were zealous for the Law?

8. Which epistle describes the Torah as "the perfect law of liberty"?

9. What does James conclude about faith that is not accompanied by deeds?

10. What evidence is there in the letter of James that believers met in synagogues?

11. Which epistle writer defines sin as transgression of the Law?

12. Which writer insisted that if you love God, you'll keep His commandments?

13. How are the righteous defined (twice) in Revelation?

14. What did Peter say about Paul's letters?

15. What does Peter claim might happen to those who misunderstand Paul's letters?

CHAPTER 12

The Message
of Paul

Many people think that Paul was the one who initiated the break from Judaism and the rejection of God's commands in Torah. Some of Paul's writings can be read that way (and have been for centuries), but as Peter noted, Paul's writings are easy to misunderstand, leading to the error of lawlessness. There is a lot of evidence in the New Testament that affirms Paul's devotion to Judaism and his obedience to Torah, and that is what we will survey here.

The pivotal point in Paul's life was a vision he received while on the way to Damascus. This vision was of Jesus confronting him for his persecution. Before the vision, Paul describes himself as a practicing Jew. He wrote, "I was advancing in Judaism beyond many of my contemporaries among my countrymen, being more extremely zealous for my ancestral traditions" (Gal. 1:14).

Many people look at Paul's Damascus road experience as a conversion from Judaism to Christianity, but it most certainly was not. Paul definitely embraced Jesus as a result of this experience, but there is no evidence to support the idea that he then stopped practicing Judaism. Instead, he accepted Jesus as Messiah and lived accordingly. Paul himself does not claim that. He never used the term "Christian," even when it was thrown in his face.

Agrippa replied to Paul, "In a short time you are going to persuade me to make a Christian of myself." And Paul said, "I would wish to God that even in a short or long time not only you, but also all who hear me this day would become such as I myself am, except for these chains." (Acts 26:28–29)

First, let's take a look at Paul before his vision. He was present at the stoning of Stephen, giving approval to his death. He was active in hunting down followers of Jesus to imprison them. Where did he find these followers of Jesus? In synagogues, of course. Paul requested letters from the chief priest to the synagogues in Damascus, so he could imprison followers of Jesus. He "went unto the high priest, and desired of him letters to Damascus to the synagogues, that if he found any of this way, whether they were men or women, he might bring them bound unto Jerusalem" (Acts 9:1b–2 KJV). This is confirmed in Paul's later testimonies at his trials, that he "went from one synagogue to another" to persecute the believers in Jesus.[1] Clearly the followers of Jesus were gathering in the synagogues on the Sabbath with other Jews, as we saw in James and as recommended in Acts 15:21.

Paul was apparently called "Saul" when he was in Hebrew or Aramaic–speaking areas, and "Paul" when he was in Greek–speaking areas. This is consistent with other people in the New Testament who are called by different names. For example, Peter is the Greek for the Hebrew Simon, just as Cephas is Aramaic. Joseph is the Hebrew equivalent of the Aramaic Barsabbas or the Greek Justus.[2]

---

1 See Acts 22:19 and 26:11.
2 See Acts 1:23.

After his vision and the blindness that followed, Paul was met and mentored by a man named Ananias, whom Paul described as "a devout man according to the law, having a good report of all the Jews which dwelt there" (Acts 22:12 KJV). There was no hint that Paul was being led to change his views on Judaism or his obedience to the Law.

How did Paul refer to his religious identity in the years after his vision in Damascus and his commission to preach Jesus to the Gentiles? He usually referred to it as "the Way," a sect of Judaism. When on trial before Felix, he said:

> But I confess this to you, that in accordance with the Way, which they call a sect, I do serve the God of our fathers, believing everything that is in accordance with the Law and is written in the Prophets; having a hope in God, which these men cherish themselves, that there shall certainly be a resurrection of both the righteous and the wicked. In view of this I also do my best to maintain a blameless conscience both before God and before other people, always. (Acts 24:14–16)

In this instance, Paul not only asserted that he followed a branch of Judaism, but simultaneously claimed to believe the essence of the teachings of Judaism. Elsewhere he was described by his opponents:

> These men, being Jews, do exceedingly trouble our city, and teach customs, which are not lawful for us to receive, neither to observe, being Romans. (Acts 16:20–21 KJV)

> For we have found this man a pestilent fellow, and a mover of sedition among all the Jews throughout the world, and a ringleader of the sect of the Nazarenes. (Acts 24:5 KJV).

The branch of Judaism (Jesus–followers) that Paul called "the Way" was also referred to as the "Nazarenes" after the man from Nazareth they followed.

One last self–identification is significant. When Paul was brought before the Sanhedrin, Paul called out, "Men and brethren, I am a Pharisee, the son of a Pharisee: of the hope and resurrection of the dead I am called in question" (Acts 23:6 KJV). Note that he didn't say, "I *was* a Pharisee." Paul still claimed to be a Pharisee. Obviously, Pharisees are a sect of Judaism. Paul referred to this in his testimony to Agrippa, when he said that the Jews accusing him "can testify, if they are willing, that according to the strictest sect of our religion, I lived as a Pharisee. And now it is because of my hope in what God has promised our fathers that I am on trial today" (Acts 26:5). Paul referred to Judaism as "our religion." Obviously, in Paul's mind, he didn't convert from Judaism to something else. He remained a faithful Jew who had been given a special commission by Jesus, the Jewish Messiah.

Throughout Acts, Paul continued to embrace Torah–obedience. An emphatic example of this is in Acts 21 when he visited the believers in Jerusalem under the leadership of James.

After we arrived in Jerusalem, the brothers and sisters received us gladly. And the following day Paul went in with us to James, and all the elders were present. After he had greeted them, he began to relate one by one the things which God had done among the Gentiles through his ministry. And when they heard about them, they began glorifying God; and they said to him, "You see, brother, how many thousands there are among the Jews of those who have believed, and they are all zealous for the Law; and they have been told about you, that you are teaching all the Jews who are among the Gentiles to abandon Moses, telling them not to circumcise their children nor to walk according to the customs. So what is to be done? They will certainly hear that you have come. Therefore, do as we tell you: we have four men who have a vow upon themselves; take them along and purify yourself together with them, and pay their expenses so that they may shave their heads; and then everyone will know that there is nothing to what they have been told about you, but that you yourself also conform, keeping the Law. (Acts 21:17–24)

Paul agreed to go through with this demonstration to silence this false rumor and show that he was living in obedience to the Law. He even paid the expenses for others to conclude their Nazirite vow, as described in Numbers 6. Acts 18:18 says Paul had taken such a vow himself as well. In any event, the believers in Jerusalem were many, and described as "thousands of Jews" who were "zealous for the law." Paul's actions were intended to prove that he was also zealous for the Law of Moses.

How did this false rumor about Paul spread? It seemed to have been based on a misunderstanding of his letter to the Galatians, which was already circulating by this time, and is commonly misunderstood. More on that later.

After Paul was arrested and put on trial several times, he repeatedly asserted that he held to the same commitment to Torah as the Jews who were accusing him. When he was first arrested and asked to speak to the crowd, he said, "I am a Jew, born in Tarsus of Cilicia, but brought up in this city, educated under Gamaliel, strictly according to the Law of our fathers, being zealous for God just as you all are today" (Acts 22:3).

We already read the statement Paul made in his trial before Felix. Two years later, he appeared before Festus and said, "I have not done anything wrong either against the Law of the Jews, or against the temple, or against Caesar" (Acts 25:8).

When on trial before Agrippa, Paul stated, "So, having obtained help from God, I stand to this day testifying both to small and great, stating nothing but what the Prophets and Moses said was going to take place" (Acts 26:22). He followed that up by asking, "King Agrippa, do you believe the Prophets? I know that you believe" (Acts 26:27).

When Paul arrived in Rome, he met with the leaders of the Jews there and stated,

> Brothers, though I had done nothing against our people or the customs of our fathers, yet I was handed over to the Romans as a prisoner from Jerusalem.... For this reason, therefore, I requested to see you and to speak with you, since I am wearing this chain for the sake of the hope of Israel. (Acts 28:17, 20)

Paul's writings, though easily misunderstood, contain plenty of statements of faithfulness to Torah.

His common theme in every defense was that he was a faithful Jew and his teaching of Jesus as Messiah fell squarely within Judaism and faithfulness to the Law and the prophets.

Paul's writings, though easily misunderstood, contain plenty of statements of faithfulness to Torah. One is slam–dunk proof for Paul's view of Torah. He wrote, "All Scripture is inspired by God and beneficial for teaching, for rebuke, for correction, for training in righteousness; so that the man or woman of God may be fully capable, equipped for every good work" (2 Timothy 3:16–17). Paul was not referring to the New Testament as that didn't exist yet. To Paul, the Scripture was the Old

Testament, the Scriptures of Judaism: the Law, Prophets, and Writings. All of it, including the Law, is profitable for several things, including instruction in righteousness, and not only for the Jew—but for "the man of God." Timothy was engaged in teaching Gentiles at Ephesus, and this was meant for him and his hearers. It's hard to imagine a more emphatic statement of Paul's faithfulness to Torah.

However, there are other similar statements too. Early in Romans, Paul made a bunch of statements that implied that Jews and Gentiles should both follow the Law that God gave through Moses.

For all who have sinned without the Law will also perish without the Law, and all who have sinned under the Law will be judged by the Law; for it is not the hearers of the Law who are righteous before God, but the doers of the Law who will be justified. For when Gentiles who do not have the Law instinctively perform the requirements of the Law, these, though not having the Law, are a law to themselves, in that they show the work of the Law written in their hearts, their conscience testifying and their thoughts alternately accusing or else defending them. (Rom. 2:12–15)

For indeed circumcision is of value if you practice the Law; but if you are a violator of the Law, your circumcision has turned into uncircumcision. So if the uncircumcised man keeps the requirements of the Law, will his uncircumcision not be regarded as circumcision? And he who is physically uncircumcised, if he keeps the Law, will he not judge you who though having the letter of the Law and circumcision are a violator of the Law? (Rom. 2:25–27)

Although speaking primarily to Jews, Paul seems to be very approving of Gentiles keeping the Law as well. At the end of chapter 3, Paul anticipated the common argument that he taught contrary to the Law. "Do we then make void the law through faith? God forbid: yea, we establish the law" (Rom. 3:31 KJV). That statement ought to be a stamp of finality regarding Paul's view of the Law.

One more point needs to be made. In Ephesians, Paul told his readers to "walk not as other Gentiles walk" (Eph. 4:17). If they are no longer to live like Gentiles, only one option remained: to live like Jews. This is what Paul expected of Gentile followers of Jesus.

Despite all these statements of Paul in support of a Torah lifestyle, most of Christianity has held that Paul taught people not to follow God's commands in Torah. They've taken this position almost unanimously since the second century. What could account for this kind of misunderstanding?

A lot of it seems to come from a misunderstanding of the epistle to the Galatians. In this letter, Paul confronted those who were teaching that Gentile followers of Jesus should formally convert to Judaism. He uses the word "circumcision" as a shorthand for the entire conversion process. Paul was not opposed to the circumcision of Jews, as he insisted Timothy be circumcised before he joined him in ministry, since Timothy's mother was a Jew.[3] In contrast, he insisted that Titus *not* be circumcised, since he was born a Gentile.[4]

This was his issue in Galatians. The prophets predicted that in the last days, people from the nations would embrace the God of Israel. If they then converted to Judaism, they would no longer be people of the nations; they would be Jews. This would defeat the purpose of people from the nations embracing the God of Israel. Paul insisted that Gentiles, who embraced Jesus as Messiah, had their sins forgiven and were on good

---

3 See Acts 16:3.

4 See Galatians 2:3.

terms with God. They didn't need to convert to Judaism. In fact, they shouldn't, because that would imply that there was something wrong with their status as believing Gentiles.

Many interpreters think that Paul was telling Gentiles that the Law was obsolete and not to be followed. It seems that much of the confusion comes from a phrase that Paul used both in Romans and Galatians. In Greek, this phrase read *erga nomou*, which on the surface is usually translated "works of law."[5] But Paul didn't seem to be using it to refer to obeying the Mosaic Law, as most translators render it.

It's clear that the Greek word *nomos*, often rendered "law," has a range of meanings.[6] In Romans 7, Paul contrasted "God's law" (in which he delights) with the "law of sin," the natural impulse to do evil.[7] The word *nomos* is used for both of these, even though the meaning is different in each case.

I am convinced that the best understanding of Paul's use of the phrase *erga nomou* has been explained by Dr. Mark Nanos.[8] He suggests that since the phrase isn't referring to keeping the Mosaic Law, but to the process of the Gentiles being circumcised and converting to Judaism, the phrase would be better translated as something like "rites of a custom." It referred to the rites that one went through (the "works") to complete the custom of conversion to Judaism. If we read Galatians with that meaning, it is much more consistent with the other statements Paul made that we have already seen. The point was that Jews should remain Jews and Gentiles should

---

5 R. David Rightmire, "What Does Works of the Law Mean? Bible Definition and References," biblestudytools.com, accessed June 2, 2023, https://www.biblestudytools.com/dictionary/works-of-the-law/.

6 James Strong, "Nomos," Strong's Greek: 3551. νόμος (NOMOS) -- that which is assigned, hence usage, law, accessed June 2, 2023, https://biblehub.com/greek/3551.htm.

7 See Romans 7:22–23.

8 Mark Nanos, "Paul's Argument Against Erga Nomou," Mark Nanos, November 23, 2021, https://marknanos.com/.

remain Gentiles. Paul discussed this concept again in 1 Corinthians.

Only, as the Lord has assigned to each one, as God has called each, in this way let him walk. And so I direct in all the churches. Was any man called when he was already circumcised? He is not to become uncircumcised. Has anyone been called in uncircumcision? He is not to be circumcised. Circumcision is nothing, and uncircumcision is nothing, but what matters is the keeping of the commandments of God. Each person is to remain in that state in which he was called. (1 Corinthians 7:17–20)

Paul summarized his conclusion in verse 19, which I would paraphrase as, "It doesn't matter if you're Jewish or Gentile; keep God's commands." This was a good summary of Paul's faithfulness to Judaism and his view on Torah observance.

Jesus and his early followers were clearly Torah–observant Jews, with the addition to their belief in the fact that Jesus was the promised Messiah and would return to rule over regathered Israel in the ultimate kingdom of God. Paul, as well as the others, held to following God's revelation and commands to His people through Moses, and Paul claimed repeatedly that he was a Jew and loyal to the Jewish Scriptures.

QUESTIONS

1. What evidence did Paul give that believers were worshiping in synagogues?

2. How do we know that Paul didn't change his religion from Judaism to something else?

3. Why did Paul, and others, go by two or more names?

4. How did Paul express the same positions as his Jewish accusers?

5. Under what circumstances did Paul claim to still be a Pharisee, the son of a Pharisee?

6. What did Paul refer to as "our religion" in his testimony to Agrippa?

7.   In Acts 21, what effort did Paul go to in order to demonstrate that he kept the Law?

8.   In his epistle to Timothy, what did Paul say was profitable for instruction in righteousness?

9.   What did Paul say in Romans 3:31 about the relationship between faith and the law?

10. What is the real topic of Paul's epistle to the Galatians?

11. Why does Dr. Mark Nanos think that "rites of a custom" is a better translation than "works of the law" and how is that significant to understanding that issue?

12. In which epistle does Paul say, in effect, that it doesn't matter if you're Jewish or Gentile, but that keeping God's commands is what counts?

Conclusion

What conclusions do you think are appropriate to draw from this examination of the Judaism taught by Jesus and his early followers? How can you implement those conclusions in your own life?

Most people these days connect following Jesus with the religion that is known as Christianity. In order to evaluate that concept, we need to recount what happened later in the first century, in the time Christianity was being established as a separate religion from Judaism.

It is well-known that the differences in religious outlook between Jews and Romans caused a lot of tension. This tension led to war in 66 C.E. and to the sacking of Jerusalem and the destruction of the temple in 70 C.E.

What is not so well-known is that after these events, the Romans imposed the previously discussed punitive tax on Jews all over the empire on men, women, and children, known as the *Fiscus Judaicus*. This meant that everyone that lived in a Jewish manner had to pay.

By this time, there were many Gentile followers of Jesus throughout the empire, trying to obey the commands of God that Jesus affirmed. However, they didn't convert to Judaism. Clearly, it would be unfair for them to be taxed as Jews when they were not officially Jews; they simply lived biblically.

If you know anything about economic incentives and the policies that create them, you could easily guess what happened as a result. Gentile followers of Jesus began to distance themselves from Judaism. They chose a different holy day from the seventh–day Sabbath that God commanded. They chose the day after the Sabbath, the day on which Jesus was raised, and started calling it "the Lord's Day." They discontinued observing the biblical feasts: Passover, Weeks (Pentecost), and Tabernacles, and instituted other holidays such as Christmas and Easter. They read Paul's writings selectively to claim that the instructions that God gave Israel through Moses were obsolete with the coming of Jesus, even though Jesus insisted that until heaven and earth pass away, the Law would be in place. They claimed that their religion was "Christianity" and the antithesis of Judaism. They also started criticizing those who tried to live biblically as having no part with Christianity.

Of course, there were still Jewish followers of Jesus who understood that their faith was still within Judaism. This group persisted for a few centuries and continued to be known as Nazarenes, but the bulk of what became Christianity distinguished itself by abandoning the commands of God and any association or respect for the people that God had chosen in the first place. Tragically, over the centuries, Christians became the foremost persecutors of the Jews. Even though Christianity has gone through reform movements, none of them came close to recovering the original Judaism that Jesus taught. In fact, Martin Luther, the great reformer, was extremely anti–Jewish. His powerful written condemnation of the Jews was reprinted when Hitler rose to power in Germany.

This transformation from a sect of Judaism to a completely separate religion called Christianity was well under way by the end of the second century. Several of the second–century church fathers said terrible things about Jews and living a Jewish (biblical) lifestyle. For example, the letter of Ignatius to the Magnesians, written in the early part of the second century, said this:[1]

> *For if we still live in according to the Jewish law, we acknowledge that we have not received grace. (8.1)*
>
> *It is absurd to profess Christ Jesus, and to Judaize (10:3)*

In his epistle to the Philadelphians, Ignatius wrote, "But if anyone preach the Jewish law unto you, listen not to him" (6:1).[2]

This is from the anonymous letter to Diognetus, probably written in the late second century:[3]

> *And next I suppose that you are especially anxious to hear why Christians do not worship in the same way as the Jews.... As for Jewish taboos with respect to food, along with their superstition about the Sabbath, their bragging about circumcision, and their hypocrisy about fast days and new moons, I hardly think that you need to be told by me that all these things are ridiculous, and*

1 Ignatius, "BibleStudyTools.Com," biblestudytools.com, accessed June 2, 2023, https://www.biblestudytools.com/history/early–church–fathers/ante–nicene/vol–1–apostolic–with–justin–martyr–irenaeus/ignatius/epistle–of–ignatius–magnesians.html.

2 Epistle of Ignatius to the Philadelphians," Wikipedia, November 30, 2021, https://en.wikipedia.org/wiki/Epistle_of_Ignatius_to_the_Philadelphians.

3 Unknown, "So–Called Letter to Diognetus," The so–called letter to diognetus, accessed June 2, 2023, https://biblehub.com/library/richardson/early_christian_fathers/the_so–called_letter_to_diognetus.htm.

not worth arguing about.... All this being so, I think that you have learned enough to see that Christians are right in holding themselves aloof from the aimlessness and trickery of Greeks and Jews alike. (3:1; 4:1, 6)

The early church councils were similarly degrading in their references about Jews and living according to the Bible. For example, the Greek historian Eusebius wrote this when Constantine wrote a letter to the bishops not present at the Council of Nicaea. One of the issues argued was the date to observe Passover/Easter.[4]

It was declared to be particularly unworthy for this, the holiest of all festivals, to follow the custom of the Jews, who had soiled their hands with the most fearful of crimes, and whose minds were blinded.... We ought not, therefore, to have anything in common with the Jews, for the Savior has shown us another way; our worship follows a more legitimate and more convenient course (the order of the days of the week); and consequently, in unanimously adopting this mode, we desire, dearest brethren, to separate ourselves from the detestable company of the Jews, for it is truly shameful for us to hear them boast that without their direction we could not keep this feast.... How, then, could we follow these Jews, who are most certainly blinded by error? For to celebrate the passover twice one year is totally inadmissible. But even if this were not so, it would still be your duty not to tarnish your soul by communications with such wicked people [the Jews]. (Vita Const., Lib. Iii., 18–20)

It's clear that by the second century, the new religion of Christianity had distanced itself from Judaism, rejecting any of the "Jewish" celebrations and modes of living that were based on the Law and the prophets. This has remained the view of most of Christianity up to the present time.

---

4 Eusebius, "Medieval Sourcebook: Constantine I: On the Keeping of Easter," Internet History Sourcebooks: Medieval Sourcebook, accessed June 2, 2023, https://sourcebooks.fordham. edu/source/const1–easter.asp.

It would seem clear that to follow Jesus today in a biblical manner needs to be done *through* Judaism. Today's Christianity is a deviant variety of what Jesus taught. Although Christianity gets some things right, it gets some important things seriously wrong. In its current form, it does not seem an appropriate venue for truly following Jesus.

On the other hand, virtually all forms of Judaism today find their identity in dismissing Jesus and his claim to be Messiah. However, they have retained the laws God gave through Moses and their understanding of the eternal covenant God made with the Jewish people.

The New Testament teaches that Christianity will someday return to loving the Father and keeping His commands, and that Israel as a people will embrace Jesus when he returns. But today both of those things seem hard to imagine.

There is a branch of Judaism that embraces Jesus as Messiah, similar to the Way of which Paul spoke. This Messianic Judaism tends to be dismissed by both traditional Judaism and Christianity for obvious reasons. It feels too Jewish to Gentile converts, so is regarded as the best place for Jewish converts only. Traditional Jews don't accept Jesus as Messiah, so that's an obvious wall for them. Nevertheless, it is perhaps the most significant way to follow Jesus within Judaism.

It's true that some Messianic congregations seem to exist only to convert Jews to Christianity, so that is not the kind of congregation a Gentile believer would want to embrace, but some Torah–observant Messianic congregations try to provide both Jews *and* Gentiles with a context in which to live and worship in a biblical manner. This is the kind of congregation to seek, if you can find one near you.

That's not always possible, but there are options. Christians, who want to continue in the church they attend, can begin to follow God's commands individually. Begin with the command to remember the Sabbath day to keep it holy, since that's one of the Ten Commandments. Decide the best way to set aside Saturday as a special day for God. Don't do regular work on that day unless you must, and take time to read the Bible. You can participate in a synagogue service online or through zoom. It's also helpful to read books from a Messianic–Jewish perspective to help you understand their thinking. It's a good idea to familiarize yourself with the Torah too, to see what other commands God gave His people that you can gradually integrate into your life. The important thing is to have a heart of love for God and a desire to obey His commands. You may be able to find groups that understand Jesus in the manner the New Testament portrays him, and meet with them too.

The important thing is to have a heart of love for God and a desire to obey His commands.

For Jews reading this, consider the possibility that when Messiah comes, He might be Joshua (Jesus), the son of Joseph, who has been here before and died and rose again. You can continue in your current synagogue if you choose, even if you conclude that you know the identity of the Messiah, but if there is a Messianic group near you, check it out.

Whoever you are, you need to realize that Jesus identified the greatest commandment as Deuteronomy 6:5: to love God with every part of your being. The New Testament writers, especially John, equated loving God with keeping His commands. The call of Jesus to repent goes out to each one of us. Which commands of God do you need to return to?

QUESTIONS

1. How would the Fiscus Judaicus give Gentile believers incentive to abandon many biblical practices?

2. What were Jewish followers of Jesus called who continued to embrace Judaism in the second and third centuries?

3. When did Christianity become a separate religion from Judaism?

4. What group has been the greatest persecutor of Jews through the centuries?

5. How did the early church councils view Judaism?

6.   Since Jesus and his early followers taught Judaism, what is necessary to truly be a follower of Jesus?

7.   What branch of Judaism today consists of followers of Jesus?

8.   What does this book recommend for Christians who truly want to follow Jesus?

9.   What does it recommend for Jews?

Appendix

Most of the Old Testament prophets wrote of the coming Messiah. The prophet Jeremiah also had plenty to say about the regathering of Israel and the establishment of his kingdom. Much of Jeremiah is about judgment, both on Israel and on surrounding nations, but there are some key passages on the coming kingdom too:

At that time they will call Jerusalem "The Throne of the Lord," and all the nations will assemble at it, at Jerusalem, for the name of the Lord; and they will no longer follow the stubbornness of their evil heart. In those days the house of Judah will walk with the house of Israel, and they will come together from the land of the north to the land that I gave your fathers as an inheritance. (Jeremiah 3:17–18)

"Behold, the days are coming," declares the Lord, "when I will raise up for David a righteous Branch; and He will reign as king and act wisely and do justice and righteousness in the land. In His days Judah will be saved, and Israel will live securely; and this is His name by which He will be called, 'The Lord Our Righteousness.' Therefore behold, the days are coming," declares the Lord, "when they will no longer say, 'As the Lord lives, who brought the sons of Israel up from the land of Egypt,' but, 'As the Lord lives, who brought up and led the descendants of the household of Israel back from the north land

and from all the countries where I had driven them.' Then they will live on their own soil." (Jeremiah 23:5–8)

"For behold, days are coming," declares the Lord, "when I will restore the fortunes of My people Israel and Judah." The Lord says, "I will also bring them back to the land that I gave to their forefathers, and they shall take possession of it.... It shall come about on that day," declares the Lord of armies, "that I will break his yoke from their necks and will tear to pieces their restraints; and strangers will no longer make them their slaves. But they shall serve the Lord their God and David their king, whom I will raise up for them. And do not fear, Jacob My servant," declares the Lord, "and do not be dismayed, Israel; for behold, I am going to save you from far away, and your descendants from the land of their captivity. And Jacob will return and be at peace, without anxiety, and no one will make him afraid." (Jeremiah 30:3, 8–10)

I will build you again and you will be rebuilt, Virgin of Israel! You will take up your tambourines again, and go out to the dances of the revelers. Again you will plant vineyards on the hills of Samaria; the planters will plant and will enjoy the fruit. For there will be a day when watchmen on the hills of Ephraim call out, "Arise, and let's go up to Zion, to the Lord our God." For this is what the Lord says:

"Sing aloud with joy for Jacob, and be joyful with the chief of the nations; proclaim, give praise, and say, 'Lord, save Your people, The remnant of Israel!' Behold, I am bringing them from the north country, and I will gather them from the remote parts of the earth, among them those who are blind and those who limp, the pregnant woman and she who is in labor, together; they will return here as a great assembly. They will come with weeping, and by pleading

I will bring them; I will lead them by streams of waters, on a straight path on which they will not stumble; for I am a father to Israel, and Ephraim is My firstborn." Hear the word of the Lord, you nations, and declare it in the coastlands far away, and say, "He who scattered Israel will gather him, and He will keep him as a shepherd keeps his flock." For the Lord has ransomed Jacob and redeemed him from the hand of him who was stronger than he. They will come and shout for joy on the height of Zion, and they will be radiant over the bounty of the Lord—over the grain, the new wine, the oil, and over the young of the flock and the herd. And their life will be like a watered garden, and they will never languish again. (Jeremiah 31:4–12)

"Behold, days are coming," declares the Lord, "when I will make a new covenant with the house of Israel and the house of Judah, not like the covenant which I made with their fathers on the day I took them by the hand to bring them out of the land of Egypt, My covenant which they broke, although I was a husband to them," declares the Lord. "For this is the covenant which I will make with the house of Israel after those days," declares the Lord: "I will put My law within them and write it on their heart; and I will be their God, and they shall be My people. They will not teach again, each one his neighbor and each one his brother, saying, 'Know the Lord,' for they will all know Me, from the least of them to the greatest of them," declares the Lord, "for I will forgive their wrongdoing, and their sin I will no longer remember." (Jeremiah 31:31–34)

As we have read, Jeremiah prophesied about the establishment of God's kingdom, the prosperity ahead, as well as the establishment of a New Covenant. For those who think that God is done with Israel, and now works only through the church, there are some key promises in chapters 31 and 33.

This is what the Lord says, He who gives the sun for light by day and the fixed order of the moon and the stars for light by night, who stirs up the sea so that its waves roar—the Lord of armies is His name: "If this fixed order departs from Me," declares the Lord, "then the descendants of Israel also will cease to be a nation before Me forever." This is what the Lord says: "If the heavens above can be measured and the foundations of the earth searched out below, then I will also reject all the descendants of Israel for everything that they have done," declares the Lord. (Jeremiah 31:35–37)

And the word of the Lord came to Jeremiah, saying, "This is what the Lord says: 'If you can break My covenant for the day and My covenant for the night, so that day and night do not occur at their proper time, then My covenant with David My servant may also be broken, so that he will not have a son to reign on his throne, and with the Levitical priests, My ministers. As the heavenly lights cannot be counted, and the sand of the sea cannot be measured, so I will multiply the descendants of My servant David and the Levites who serve Me.'" And the word of the Lord came to Jeremiah, saying, "Have you not observed what these people have asserted, saying, 'The two families which the Lord chose, He has rejected them'? So they despise My people as no longer being a nation in their sight. This is what the Lord says: 'If My covenant for day and night does not continue, and I have not established the fixed patterns of heaven and earth, then I would reject the descendants of Jacob and David My servant, so as not to take from his descendants rulers over the descendants of Abraham, Isaac, and Jacob. But I will restore their fortunes and have mercy on them.'" (Jeremiah 33:19–26)

"Behold, days are coming," declares the Lord, "when I will fulfill the good word which I have spoken concerning the house of Israel and the house of Judah. In

those days and at that time I will make a righteous Branch of David sprout; and He shall execute justice and righteousness on the earth. In those days Judah will be saved and Jerusalem will live in safety; and this is the name by which it will be called: the Lord is our righteousness." For this is what the Lord says: "David shall not lack a man to sit on the throne of the house of Israel." (Jeremiah 33:14–17)

The Jews are included in God's plan to the end. God has no intention of just saving the Christian church. He is returning for Jew and Gentile alike, and in one body, not two separate ones. One Lord, one faith, one body.

> *He is returning for Jew and Gentile alike, and in one body, not two separate ones.*

The prophecy of Ezekiel also has much to say about the restoration of Israel. In chapter 11, we read,

Therefore say, "This is what the Lord God says: 'I will gather you from the peoples and assemble you from the countries among which you have been scattered, and I will give you the land of Israel.'" When they come there, they will remove all its detestable things and all its abominations from it. And I will give them one heart, and put a new spirit within them. And I will remove the heart of stone from their flesh and give them a heart of flesh, so that they may walk in My statutes, and keep My ordinances and do them. Then they will be My people, and I shall be their God. (Ezekiel 11:17–20)

In chapter 34, God likens the people of Israel to sheep, and their leaders to shepherds.

"Therefore, I will save My flock, and they will no longer be plunder; and I will judge between one sheep and another. Then I will appoint over them one shepherd, My servant David, and he will feed them; he will feed them himself and be their shepherd. And I, the Lord, will be their God, and My servant David will be prince among them; I the Lord have spoken. And I will make a covenant of peace with them and eliminate harmful animals from the land, so that they may live securely in the wilderness and sleep in the woods. I will make them and the places around My hill a blessing. And I will make showers fall in their season; they will be showers of blessing. Also the tree of the field will yield its fruit and the earth will yield its produce, and they will be secure on their land. Then they will know that I am the Lord, when I have broken the bars of their yoke and have saved them from the hand of those who enslaved them. They will no longer be plunder to the nations, and the animals of the earth will not devour them; but they will live securely, and no one will make them afraid. I will establish for them a renowned planting place, and they will not again be victims of famine in the land, and they will not endure the insults of the nations anymore. Then they will know that I, the Lord their God, am with them, and that they, the house of Israel, are My people," declares the Lord God. "As for you, My sheep, the sheep of My pasture, you are mankind, and I am your God," declares the Lord God. (Ezekiel 34:22–31)

The entirety of chapter 36 is about the restoration of Israel, the heart of it in verses 22–29:

Therefore say to the house of Israel, '"This is what the Lord God says: 'It is not for your sake, house of Israel, that I am about to act, but for My holy name, which you have profaned among the nations where you went. And I will vindicate the holiness of My great name which has been profaned among the nations, which you have profaned among them. Then the nations will know that I am the Lord,' declares the Lord God, 'when I show Myself holy among you in their sight. For I will take you from the nations, and gather you from all the lands; and I will bring you into your own land. Then I will sprinkle clean water on you, and you will be clean; I will cleanse you from all your filthiness and from all your idols. Moreover, I will give you a new heart and put a new spirit within you; and I will remove the heart of stone from your flesh and give you a heart of flesh. And I will put My Spirit within you and bring it about that you walk in My statutes, and are careful and follow My ordinances. And you will live in the land that I gave to your forefathers; so you will be My people, and I will be your God. Moreover, I will save you from all your uncleanness; and I will call for the grain and multiply it, and I will not bring a famine on you.'" (Ezekiel 36:22–29)

Ezekiel 37 contains the famous vision of the valley of dry bones, which represent the people of Israel. God shows him the valley full of bones and directly tells Ezekiel that these bones *are the nation Israel,* a nation He intends to raise up and restore unto Himself.

The hand of the Lord was upon me, and He brought me out by the Spirit of the Lord and set me down in the middle of the valley; and it was full of bones. He had me pass among them all around, and behold, there were very many on the surface of the valley; and behold, they were very dry. Then He said to me, "Son of man, can these bones live?" And I answered, "Lord God, You Yourself know." Again He said to me, "Prophesy over these bones and say to them, 'You dry bones, hear the word of the Lord.' This is what the Lord God says to these bones: 'Behold, I am going to make breath enter you so that you may come to life. And I will attach tendons to you, make flesh grow back on you, cover you with skin, and put breath in you so that you may come to life; and you will know that I am the Lord.'" So I prophesied as I was commanded; and as I prophesied, there was a loud noise, and behold, a rattling; and the bones came together, bone to its bone. And I looked, and behold, tendons were on them, and flesh grew and skin covered them; but there was no breath in them. Then He said to me, "Prophesy to the breath, prophesy, son of man, and say to the breath, 'The Lord God says this: "Come from the four winds, breath, and breathe on these slain, so that they come to life."'" So I prophesied as He commanded me, and the breath entered them, and they came to life and stood on their feet, an exceedingly great army. Then He said to me, "Son of man, these bones are the entire house of Israel; behold, they say, 'Our bones are dried up and our hope has perished. We are completely cut off.' Therefore prophesy and say to them, 'This is what the Lord God says: "Behold, I am going to open your graves and cause you to come up out of your graves, My people; and I will bring you into the land of Israel. Then you will know that I am the Lord, when I have opened your graves and caused you to come up out of your graves, My people. And I will put My Spirit within you and you will come to life, and I will place you on your own land. Then you will know that I, the Lord, have spoken and done it,"'" declares the Lord. (Ezekiel 37:1–14)

Later in the chapter we have further details of the kingdom that God will set up.

And say to them, "This is what the Lord God says: 'Behold, I am going to take the sons of Israel from among the nations where they have gone, and I will gather them from every side and bring them into their own land; and I will make them one nation in the land, on the mountains of Israel; and one king will be king for all of them; and they will no longer be two nations, and no longer be divided into two kingdoms. They will no longer defile themselves with their idols, or with their detestable things, or with any of their offenses; but I will rescue them from all their dwelling places in which they have sinned, and will cleanse them. And they will be My people, and I will be their God. And My servant David will be king over them, and they will all have one shepherd; and they will walk in My ordinances, and keep My statutes and follow them. And they will live on the land that I gave to My servant Jacob, in which your fathers lived; and they will live on it, they, and their sons and their sons' sons, forever; and My servant David will be their leader forever. And I will make a covenant of peace with them; it will be an everlasting covenant with them. And I will place them and multiply them, and set My sanctuary in their midst forever. My dwelling place also will be among them; and I will be their God, and they will be My people. And the nations will know that I am the Lord who sanctifies Israel, when My sanctuary is in their midst forever."' (Ezekiel 37:21–28)

Daniel also has a couple of references to this future kingdom, although in a different and more historical context. Daniel interprets King Nebuchadnezzar's dream:

As for you, O king, while on your bed your thoughts turned to what would take place in the future; and He who reveals secrets has made known to you what will take place. But as for me, this secret has not been revealed to me for any wisdom residing in me more than in any other living person, but for the purpose of making the interpretation known to the king, and that you may understand the thoughts of your mind. You, O king, were watching and behold, there was a single great statue; that statue, which was large and of extraordinary radiance, was standing in front of you, and its appearance was awesome. The head of that statue was made of fine gold, its chest and its arms of silver, its belly and its thighs of bronze, its legs of iron, and its feet partly of iron and partly of clay. You continued watching until a stone was broken off without hands, and it struck the statue on its feet of iron and clay, and crushed them. Then the iron, the clay, the bronze, the silver, and the gold were crushed to pieces all at the same time, and they were like chaff from the summer threshing floors; and the wind carried them away so that not a trace of them was found. But the stone that struck the statue became a great mountain and filled the entire earth. This was the dream; and now we will tell its interpretation before the king. You, O king, are the king of kings, to whom the God of heaven has given the kingdom, the power, the strength, and the honor; and wherever the sons of mankind live, or the animals of the field, or the birds of the sky, He has handed them over to you and has made you ruler over them all. You are the head of gold. And after you another kingdom will arise inferior to you, then another third kingdom of bronze, which will rule over all the earth. Then there will be a fourth kingdom as strong as iron; just as iron smashes and crushes everything, so, like iron that crushes, it will smash and crush all these things. And in that you saw the feet and toes, partly of potter's clay and partly of iron, it will be a divided kingdom; but it will have within it some of the toughness of iron, since you saw the iron mixed with common clay. And just as the toes of the feet were partly of iron and partly of pottery, so some of the kingdom will be strong, and part of it will be fragile. In that you saw the iron mixed with common clay, they will combine with one another in their descendants; but they will not adhere to one another, just as iron does not combine with pottery. And in the days of those kings the God of heaven will set up a kingdom which will never be destroyed, and that kingdom will not be left for another people; it will crush and put an end to all these kingdoms, but it will itself endure forever. (Dan. 2:29–44)

In chapter 7, Daniel had a dream of his own:

In the first year of Belshazzar king of Babylon, Daniel saw a dream and visions in his mind as he lay on his bed; then he wrote the dream down and told the following summary of it. Daniel said, "I was looking in my vision by night, and behold, the four winds of heaven were stirring up the great sea. And four great beasts were coming up from the sea, different from one another. The first was like a lion but had the wings of an eagle. I kept looking until its wings were plucked, and it was lifted up from the ground and set up on two feet like a man; a human mind also was given to it. And behold, another beast, a second one, resembling a bear. And it was raised up on one side, and three ribs were in its mouth between its teeth; and they said this to it: 'Arise, devour much meat!' After this I kept looking, and behold, another one, like a leopard, which had on its back four wings of a bird; the beast also had four heads, and dominion was given to it. After this I kept looking in the night visions, and behold, a fourth beast, dreadful and terrible, and extremely strong; and it had large iron teeth. It devoured and crushed, and trampled down the remainder with its feet; and it was different from all the beasts that were before it, and it had ten horns. While I was thinking about the horns, behold, another horn, a little one, came up among them, and three of the previous horns were plucked out before it; and behold, this horn possessed eyes like human eyes, and a mouth uttering great boasts.

I kept looking until thrones were set up, and the Ancient of Days took His seat; His garment was white as snow, and the hair of His head like pure wool His throne was ablaze with flames, its wheels were a burning fire. A river of fire was flowing and coming out from before Him; thousands upon thousands were serving Him, and myriads upon myriads were standing before Him; the court convened, and the books were opened.

"Then I kept looking because of the sound of the boastful words which the horn was speaking; I kept looking until the beast was killed, and its body was destroyed and given to the burning fire. As for the rest of the beasts, their dominion was taken away, but an extension of life was granted to them for an appointed period of time.

"I kept looking in the night visions, and behold, with the clouds of heaven one like a son of man was coming, and He came up to the Ancient of Days and was presented before Him. And to Him was given dominion, honor, and a kingdom, so that all the peoples, nations, and populations of all languages might serve Him. His dominion is an everlasting dominion which will not pass away; and His kingdom is one which will not be destroyed.

"As for me, Daniel, my spirit was distressed within me, and the visions in my mind kept alarming me. I approached one of those who were standing by and began requesting of him the exact meaning of all this. So he told me and made known to me the interpretation of these things: 'These great beasts, which are four in number, are four kings who will arise from the earth. But the saints of the Highest One will receive the kingdom and take possession of the kingdom forever, for all ages to come.'

"Then I desired to know the exact meaning of the fourth beast, which was different from all the others, exceedingly dreadful, with its teeth of iron and its claws of bronze, and which devoured, crushed, and trampled down the remainder with its feet, and the meaning of the ten horns that were on its

head, and the other horn which came up, and before which three of the horns fell, namely, that horn which had eyes and a mouth uttering great boasts, and which was larger in appearance than its associates. I kept looking, and that horn was waging war with the saints and prevailing against them, until the Ancient of Days came and judgment was passed in favor of the saints of the Highest One, and the time arrived when the saints took possession of the kingdom.

"This is what he said: 'The fourth beast will be a fourth kingdom on the earth which will be different from all the other kingdoms, and will devour the whole earth and trample it down and crush it. As for the ten horns, out of this king–dom ten kings will arise; and another will arise after them, and he will be different from the previous ones and will humble three kings. And he will speak against the Most High and wear down the saints of the Highest One, and he will intend to make alterations in times and in law; and they will be handed over to him for a time, times, and half a time. But the court will convene for judgment, and his dominion will be taken away, annihilated and destroyed forever. Then the sovereignty, the dominion, and the greatness of all the kingdoms under the whole heaven will be given to the people of the saints of the Highest One; His kingdom will be an everlasting kingdom, and all the empires will serve and obey Him.' At this point the revelation ended. As for me, Daniel, my thoughts were greatly alarming me and my face became pale, but I kept the matter to myself." (Dan. 7:1–29)

Daniel gave an interpretation of the dream which included these phrases: "but the saints of the most High shall take the kingdom, and possess the kingdom for ever, even for ever and ever" (Dan. 7:18 KJV).

But the court will convene for judgment, and his [the little horn's] dominion will be taken away, annihilated and destroyed forever. Then the sovereignty, the dominion, and the greatness of all the kingdoms under the whole heaven will be given to the people of the saints of the Highest One; His kingdom will be an everlasting kingdom, and all the empires will serve and obey Him. (Dan. 7:26–27, addition mine)

This dream is the source for the title, "Son of Man," which Jesus often used to describe himself. The basic meaning of the phrase is "a human one"; but in this place, it referred to a specific human to whom God would give dominion and authority over all people forever. Jesus claimed to be that One.

The Minor Prophets also talked about this future kingdom, although not as extensively. Hosea mentioned it briefly in two passages.

Yet the number of the sons of Israel will be like the sand of the sea, which cannot be measured or counted; and in the place where it is said to them, "You are not My people," it will be said to them, "You are the sons of the living God." And the sons of Judah and the sons of Israel will be gathered together, and they will appoint for themselves one leader, and they will go up from the land, for the day of Jezreel will be great. (Hosea 1:10–11)

For the sons of Israel will live for many days without a king or leader, without sacrifice or memorial stone, and without ephod or household idols. Afterward the sons of Israel will return and seek the Lord their God and David their king; and they will come trembling to the Lord and to His goodness in the last days. (Hosea 3:4–5)

The prophetic book of Joel ends with the following account:

Beat your plowshares into swords, and your pruning hooks into spears; let the weak man say, "I am a warrior." Hurry and come, all you surrounding nations, and gather yourselves there. Bring down, Lord, Your warriors. Let the nations be awakened and come up to the Valley of Jehoshaphat, for there I will sit to judge all the surrounding nations. Put in the sickle, for the harvest is ripe. Come, tread the grapes, for the wine press is full; the vats overflow, for their wickedness is great.

Multitudes, multitudes in the valley of decision! For the day of the Lord is near in the valley of decision. The sun and moon have become dark, and the stars have lost their brightness. The Lord roars from Zion and utters His voice from Jerusalem, and the heavens and the earth quake. But the Lord is a refuge for His people, and a stronghold for the sons of Israel.

Then you will know that I am the Lord your God, dwelling on Zion, My holy mountain. So Jerusalem will be holy, and strangers will no longer pass through it. And on that day the mountains will drip with sweet wine, and the hills will flow with milk, and all the brooks of Judah will flow with water; and a spring will go out from the house of the Lord and water the Valley of Shittim.

Egypt will become a wasteland, and Edom will become a desolate wilderness, because of the violence done to the sons of Judah, in whose land they have shed innocent blood. But Judah will be inhabited forever, and Jerusalem for all generations. And I will avenge their blood which I have not avenged, for the Lord dwells in Zion. (Joel 3:10–21)

Amos ends with this:

"On that day I will raise up the fallen shelter of David, and wall up its gaps; I will also raise up its ruins and rebuild it as in the days of old; so that they may possess the remnant of Edom and all the nations who are called by My name," declares the Lord who does this.

"Behold, days are coming," declares the Lord, "when the plowman will overtake the reaper, and the one who treads grapes will overtake him who sows the seed; when the mountains will drip grape juice, and all the hills will come apart. I will also restore the fortunes of My people Israel, and they will rebuild the desolated cities and live in them; they will also plant vineyards and drink their wine, and make gardens and eat their fruit. I will also plant them on their land, and they will not be uprooted again from their land which I have given them," says the Lord your God. (Amos 9:11–15)

Obadiah, which contains only one chapter, doesn't say much, but finishes thus:

And the exiles of this army of the sons of Israel, who are among the Canaanites as far as Zarephath, and the exiles of Jerusalem who are in Sepharad, will possess the cities of the Negev. The deliverers will ascend Mount Zion to judge the mountain of Esau, and the kingdom will be the Lord's. (Obadiah 20–21)

Micah repeats a passage from Isaiah 2:

And it will come about in the last days that the mountain of the house of the Lord will be established as the chief of the mountains. It will be raised above the hills, and the peoples will stream to it. Many nations will come and say, "Come and let's go up to the mountain of the Lord and to the house of the God of Jacob, so that He may teach us about His ways, and that we may walk in His paths." For from Zion will go forth the law, and the word of the Lord from Jerusalem. And He will judge between many peoples and render decisions for mighty, distant nations. Then they will beat their swords into plowshares, and their spears into pruning hooks; nation will not lift a sword against nation, and never again will they train for war. Instead, each of them will sit under his vine and under his fig tree, with no one to make them afraid, because the mouth of the Lord of armies has spoken. (Micah 4:1–4)

As previously mentioned, Micah 5:2–5a is the source of the prophecy about a ruler coming from Bethlehem, the city of David. Nahum makes only one brief mention: "Behold, on the mountains, the feet of him who brings good news, who announces peace! Celebrate your feasts, Judah, pay your vows. For never again will the wicked one pass through you; he is eliminated completely" (Nah. 1:15).

Habakkuk cites Isaiah: "For the earth will be filled with the knowledge of the glory of the Lord, as the waters cover the sea" (Hab. 2:14).

Zephaniah writes of the rejoicing of Israel when God's kingdom is established:

Shout for joy, daughter of Zion! Shout in triumph, Israel! Rejoice and triumph with all your heart, daughter of Jerusalem! The Lord has taken away His judgments against you, He has cleared away your enemies. The King of Israel, the Lord, is in your midst; you will no longer fear disaster. On that day it will be said to Jerusalem: "Do not be afraid, Zion; do not let your hands fall limp. The Lord your God is in your midst, a victorious warrior. He will rejoice over you with joy, He will be quiet in His love, He will rejoice over you with shouts of joy. I will gather those who are worried about the appointed feasts—they came from you, Zion; the disgrace of exile is a burden on them.

"Behold, I am going to deal at that time with all your oppressors; I will save those who limp and gather the scattered, and I will turn their shame into praise and fame in all the earth. At that time I will bring you in, even at the time when I gather you together; indeed, I will make you famous and praiseworthy among all the peoples of the earth, when I restore your fortunes before your eyes," says the Lord. (Zephaniah 3:14–20)

Haggai makes this short declaration:

For this is what the Lord of armies says: "Once more in a little while, I am going to shake the heavens and the earth, the sea also and the dry land. I will shake all the nations; and they will come with the wealth of all nations, and I will fill this house with glory," says the Lord of armies. "The silver is Mine and the gold is Mine," declares the Lord of armies. "The latter glory of this house will be greater than the former," says the Lord of armies, "and in this place I will give peace," declares the Lord of armies. (Haggai 2:6–9)

Zechariah goes into more detail than the others. The entirety of chapter 8 deals with this future time of blessing. Here is a sample:

Then the word of the Lord of armies came, saying, "The Lord of armies says this: 'I am exceedingly jealous for Zion, yes, with great wrath I am jealous for her.' The Lord says this: 'I will return to Zion and dwell in the midst of Jerusalem. Then Jerusalem will be called the City of Truth, and the mountain of the Lord of armies will be called the Holy Mountain.' The Lord of armies says this: 'Old men and old women will again sit in the public squares of Jerusalem, each person with his staff in his hand because of age. And the public squares of the city will be filled with boys and girls playing in its squares.' The Lord of armies says this: 'If it is too difficult in the sight of the remnant of this people in those days, will it also be too difficult in My sight?' declares the Lord of armies. The Lord of armies says this: 'Behold, I am going to save My people from the land of the east and from the land of the west; and I will bring them back and they will live in the midst of Jerusalem; and they shall be My people, and I will be their God in truth and righteousness.'" (Zech. 8:1–8)

Most of Zechariah 9 and 10 also relate to this time.

Rejoice greatly, daughter of Zion! Shout in triumph, daughter of Jerusalem! Behold, your king is coming to you; He is righteous and endowed with salvation, humble, and mounted on a donkey, even on a colt, the foal of a donkey. And I will eliminate the chariot from Ephraim and the horse from Jerusalem; and the bow of war will be eliminated. And He will speak peace to the nations; and His dominion will be from sea to sea, and from the Euphrates River to the ends of the earth. (Zech. 9:9–10)

And the Lord shall be seen over them, and his arrow shall go forth as the lightning: and the Lord God shall blow the trumpet, and shall go with whirlwinds of the south. The Lord of hosts shall defend them; and they shall devour, and subdue with sling stones; and they shall drink, and make a noise as through wine; and they shall be filled like bowls, and as the corners of the altar. And the Lord their God shall save them in that day as the flock of his people: for they shall be as the stones of a crown, lifted up as an ensign upon his land. (Zech. 9:14–16)

The final chapter devotes itself to the victory of the Lord at that time:

Then the Lord will go forth and fight against those nations, as when He fights on a day of battle. On that day His feet will stand on the Mount of Olives, which is in front of Jerusalem on the east; and the Mount of Olives will be split in its middle from east to west forming a very large valley. Half of the mountain will move toward the north, and the other half toward the south. And you will flee by the valley of My mountains, for the valley of the mountains will reach to Azel; yes, you will flee just as you fled from the earthquake in the days of Uzziah king of Judah. Then the Lord, my God, will come, and all the holy ones with Him.... And the Lord will be King over all the earth; on that day the Lord will be the only one, and His name the only one.... Then it will come about that any who are left of all the nations that came against Jerusalem will go up from year to year to worship the King, the Lord of armies, and to celebrate the Feast of Booths, and it will be that whichever of the families of the earth does not go up to Jerusalem to worship the King, the Lord of armies, there will be no rain on them. (Zech. 14:3–5, 9,16–17).

The book of Malachi ends with a short chapter about the last days:

"For behold, the day is coming, burning like a furnace; and all the arrogant and every evildoer will be chaff; and the day that is coming will set them ablaze," says the Lord of armies, "so that it will leave them neither root nor branches. But for you who fear My name, the sun of righteousness will rise with healing in its wings; and you will go forth and frolic like calves from the stall. And you will crush the wicked underfoot, for they will be ashes under the soles of your feet on the day that I am preparing," says the Lord of armies. "Remember the Law of Moses My servant, the statutes and ordinances which I commanded him in Horeb for all Israel. Behold, I am going to send you Elijah the prophet before the coming of the great and terrible day of the Lord. He will turn the hearts of the fathers back to their children and the hearts of the children to their fathers, so that I will not come and strike the land with complete destruction." (Malachi 4:1–6)

As you can see, most of the detail is given in the writings of Isaiah, Jeremiah, and Ezekiel, but the establishment of God's kingdom is a constant refrain throughout. Eventually the scattered people of Israel would be brought back to the land God promised them, and God would establish His kingdom, centered in Jerusalem and ruled by a human descendant of David: the Messiah. This would be a time of tremendous peace and prosperity when the knowledge of God would be universal and God's commands and decrees would be internalized and obeyed. This Davidic King Messiah will rule, not only over Jews, but over the nations of the earth as well—over all that embraced the God of Israel and His instructions. This is the hope which pervades Judaism today, just as it did during the first century. This is the hope Jesus came to fulfill. He declared himself the King and the Bringer of his kingdom, and if the leadership of the people of that time hadn't rejected him, he would have done it already.